Creating a Nonviolent Culture in a Modern Organization

Miriam Baermann
and
Stephen A. Engelking

Creating a Nonviolent Culture in a Modern Organization

© 2013 Miriam Baermann and Stephen A. Engelking

© 2023 Second Edition Published by Texianer Verlag

Johannesstrasse 12 D-78609 Tuningen Germany

ISBN-13: 978-3-910667-03-7

Cover illustration: English: Team work by Japuraalwis Licensed under the Creative Commons Attribution-Share Alike 3.0 Unported license.
https://commons.wikimedia.org/wiki/File:Team_work.jpg

Table of Contents

Introduction   9
Explanatory notes on the terms employed   12

Culture   13
The cultural situation in the current century   13
The definition of culture in organizations   14
Deal and Kennedy's cultural model   17
Coherence of national culture and organizational culture   21
The ecological and social need for cultural change   25
The link between culture in organizations and societies   32
The difference between culture and structure   34
The exertion of influence on organizational culture   36
Aspects of culture in the investigated organization   38

Violence vs. Nonviolence   41
Definitions of violence   41
Causes of violence   42
Violence against animals and the environment   48
The destructive effect of violence in organizations   49
Violence in language   52
A definition of nonviolence based on Gandhi's thinking   55
The nonviolent culture   62

Leadership for a Nonviolent Culture   69
Vision   70
Motivational models   80
Nonviolent use of power   88

The nonviolent use of money	91
Servant leadership	93
Principle-centered leadership	95
Conflict management	104
Nonviolent communication based on Marshall Rosenberg	107
The Learning Organization	119
Conclusion about influencing culture through leadership	129
Critical Summary	**131**
Bibliography	**133**
Appendices	**141**
Appendix A – The Work With Questionnaires	143
Appendix B – Survey 1	145
Appendix C – Survey 2	153
Appendix D – Survey 3	155
Appendix E – Survey 4	161
Appendix F – Principles of the Mondcivitan Republic	169
Appendix G - Documentation of the Researcher's Experiences	175
Index	**187**

List of Diagrams

Fig. 1: Composition of Organizational culture. (Based on Schein (1995) p. 30.)   16

Fig. 2: Culture model of Deal and Kennedy (Based on Deal and Kennedy (1982) p. 108).   20

Fig. 3: Engagement Index in Germany 2008 (Based on Kleine (2009) p. 1.)   28

Fig. 4: Engagement Index of the Investigated Company. Survey 1, App. B.   30

Fig. 5: Productivity study 2002: Reasons for productivity loss in organizations worldwide (Based on Proudfoot consulting (2002) p. 9.)   31

Fig. 6: The IGOS. Adapted from Engelking (2012, p.39).   33

Fig. 7: Degree of agreement that commerce without morality leads to violence. Survey 3, app. D.   45

Fig. 8: Agreement degree on whether talents should be used for the welfare of all. Survey 3, app. D.   58

Fig. 9: Opinions on mistakes. Survey 3, app. D.   67

Fig. 10: Creative tension with shared vision. (Based on Senge (1990) p. 151.)   78

Fig. 11: Maslow's pyramid of needs with Herzberg's motivation-hygiene theory. (Based on Maslow, quoted in Lorenz and Rohrschneider (2007) p. 84.)   80

Fig. 12: Effort and Gain in an ideal state (left) and in a usual state (right). (Based on Lorenz and Rohrschneider (2007) p. 89.)   87

Fig. 13: Effort and gain model in a status of employee's dissatisfaction. (Based on Lorenz and Rohrschneider (2007) p. 90.)   87

Fig. 14: Alternative center of a principle centered organization. (Based on Covey (2003) p. 24.)   98

Fig. 15: Pyramid of influence. (Based on Covey (2003) p. 119.)   102

Fig. 16: Evaluation of the question "How do you see your function as an ideal?" cf. Survey 2, app. C.   104

Fig. 17: Evaluation on statement "Nonviolent communication is efficient because it prevents misunderstandings and ease conflicts". Survey 4, app. E.   111

Fig. 18: Based on Egyptian (2009) p. 13, adapted from Blaine 1996.)   118

Fig. 19: Evaluation of learning disability investigated according to Senge's definition. cf. App. I.   126

List of Tables

Table 1: Examples of dominance strategies in language *(Lindemann and Heim. 2010, p. 32-33.)*   53

Table 2: Evaluation of dominance strategies in language cf. Survey 3, app. D.   54

Table 3: Hygiene factors and motivation factors according to Herzberg's two factor theory. (Based on Herzberg, quoted in Lorenz / Rohrschneider (2007) p. 86.)   82

Table 4: Principles friendly environment according to Greenleaf and its development at the company under investigation. (Based on Greenleaf (2003) p. 33.)   94

Table 5: The four kinds of receiving a message. (Based on Lindemann and Heim (2010) p. 101.)   115

Table 6: Principles of the Mondcivitan Republic. (Based on Schonfield (2012) pp. 226-227.   174

Introduction

Increasing violence amongst youth in society, burn-out as a widespread disease and scandals in companies are only some of the headlines which appear regularly in the news media. Politics scarcely seems to have any success in fighting violence and injustice in society or in the world. The suggestion made by this book is that people do not have to wait for a political leader to save them but that everyone can contribute to a less violent, more peaceful and just world.

It will be demonstrated that organizations have an enormous influence on society and we will consider the possibilities which an organization has to contribute to a less violent culture. By the term *organization* all forms of organized groups of people who come together for a common purpose are meant and it includes, for example, schools, clubs, charities and social services. For the purpose of this book, we will mainly concentrate on companies.

The intention is to focus particularly on the issues related to the theme of creating a nonviolent culture in the workplace. In the first section on culture we deal with several questions regarding culture, including such fundamental questions as *What is organizational culture?*, *What are the dimensions of culture?* and *Is it possible to influence it and if yes, how does it work?*

In the second part, we take a look at the terms *violence* and *nonviolence* and a survey carried out on how these aspects occur in society and organizations.

The third part is the largest and deals with the qualities of leadership and with the organizational conditions which are necessary to create a nonviolent culture.

We hope it will become clearer to the reader that nonviolence is not a strategy or a formula to be used as needed. It can appear very different in different situations. There are component elements which can promote it and there are certain principles that cannot be violated if one wishes to establish true nonviolence. Nevertheless, there is no one patent formula nor one exclusively correct way of creating a nonviolent culture. It requires considerable creativity and endurance to establish and can take a variety of forms.

A (nonviolent) culture has so many facets that there can be no claim to exhaustiveness and that is not a considered aim here. Those aspects of creating a nonviolent culture have been chosen which are considered important for most organizations regardless of their type. Another criteria for choosing the subjects was that they could be verified by first hand experience. An additional aspect which was considered was that the more generally applicable elements should be discussed allowing for the consideration of alternative viewpoints. For example, the family is a very important social unit for human beings and has a great influence on the development of violence in society. Therefore a family friendly organizational structure must be an integral part of a nonviolent culture. However, this aspect has only been mentioned briefly because it evolves in essence from the more general need to create structures which are able to meet people's needs.

Our main aim is to give a first impression of what can be understood by a nonviolent culture and how this can affect the performance of an organization and the society within which it operates. It demonstrates the fact that every person can influence an organization and society by changing himself. Gandhi appeals for "being the change you want to see in the world" which is a core theme of this book and was at the outset, the motivation for taking a closer look at the topic of a nonviolent culture.

To underpin the theory of nonviolence in the workplace, research lasting three months was carried out in a medium sized organization in the machine industry in Southern Germany. This is not intended by any means to be considered as exhaustive research but rather an example of how such further research could be carried out.

Explanatory notes on the terms employed

In this work, when writing generally about persons such as a leader, the male forms *he, him, himself...* are used for the sake of simplification. Nevertheless, always both sexes are meant, both male and female without any inference or assumption.

Another stylistic matter is the use of the term *employee*. When referring to companies as a form of organization, this term is often adequate but may not be so for other organizational forms also referred to here. Even when talking about companies it might be preferable to use the term *organizational member* instead of *employee* because the term *employee* indicates some form of hierarchy which may not necessarily be applicable even to a conventional company. Having stated that, the word *employee* is used where it has been deemed appropriate.

Finally, the words *nonviolence* and *nonviolent* require some consideration. In the English language these words are usually written as *non-violence* or *non-violent*. However, because *nonviolence* does not simply mean the absence of violence it is a novel concept which for this reason will be written without a hyphen.

Culture

The cultural situation in the current century

Wilber (2001, p.1) points out a significant aspect of the culture of the current century. He calls attention to the phenomena that all cultures of the world, past and present, are available to a certain extent to everybody, something which has not happened before.

Senge (1990, p.3) discusses the issue that in western society, people learn to fragment the world from a very early age. The holistic view of the binding connection between all things has become lost and with it, the awareness of the consequences arising from personal actions. Today, people are more interconnected than ever before and there is therefore almost no action which does not affect someone else (Handy, 1999).

Lyberth (2008) discusses this problem from a different point of view. According to him, modern society is trapped in a limiting belief system. He makes the comparison with the tree of knowledge where every being focuses on only one specific branch as being the correct belief system, forgetting that this tree has hundreds and thousands of other branches. By identifying with only one single branch, the rest of the tree is left to die. Everywhere in the world people will sing the same songs, pray to the same God, have the same ideals, and wear the same clothes. Sooner or later, this single branch on the dead tree will die as well—a suicidal program (Lyberth, 2008, p.70).

The definition of culture in organizations

An organization's culture is something very complex and a subject which has occupied the thoughts of many writers and thinkers who have arrived at equally different opinions. The study of organizational culture has become very popular because the different models offer explanations about the difference of performance between organizations, of their members and of their overall efficiency. Schwarz and Davis (1981) define organizational culture as the following: "Culture is a pattern of beliefs and expectations shared by the organization's members. These beliefs and expectations produce norms that powerfully shape the behavior of individuals and groups within the organization" (p.33). A similar definition is made by Edgar Schein (2004) who states that organizational culture is "a pattern of shared basic assumptions that the group learned as it solved its problems of external adaptation and internal integration that has worked well enough to be considered valid, and therefore, to be taught to new members as the correct way to perceive, think, and feel in relation to those problems"(p.17). Besides, Schein defines three different levels of culture (p.30-33):

Artifacts

Artifacts are superficial. They include the visible structures, processes and products in an organization. Artifacts are visible to everyone whilst not so easy to decipher.

Espoused Values

Espoused values are constituted justifications through existing strategies, aims and the philosophy of an organization. They are based on the values of a particular individual who will be accepted as the leader if he can get the group to solve problems using his directions. This person's values will become manifest in the organization.

Basic Assumptions

Basic assumptions are fundamental and self-evident assumptions, perceptions, thoughts and emotions. They are the basis for values and action within the organization. Basic assumptions evolve as a solution to a certain problem proves to have worked several times. Group members will automatically act according to their basic assumptions in order to try to make their environment stable and predictable.

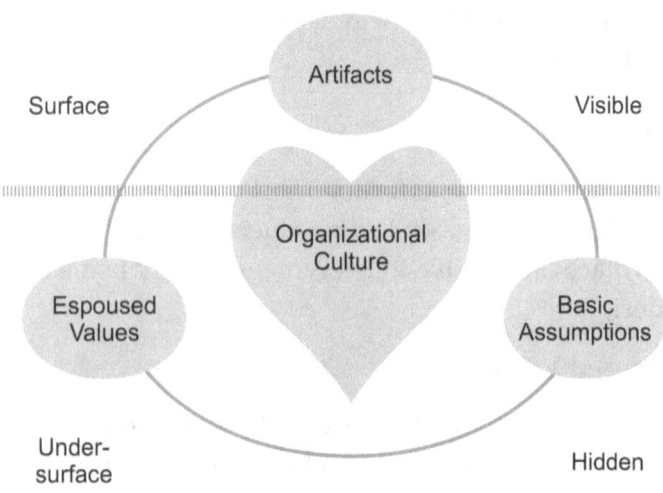

Fig. 1: Composition of Organizational culture. (Based on Schein (1995) p. 30.)

Artifacts at an investigated company were found to be, for example, courses of action but it is difficult to know what they tell us about the culture of the individual departments. The espoused values also vary between the departments. Often, these are not evident until the person who created them leaves the department or the company, and the absence of his actions becomes obvious. For example, Person A always ensures that the light is turned off each evening before he leaves work. Not until Person A is gone will people realize that it was he who always switched off the light. This action was driven by certain values this person brought into the company, such as to be careful not to waste resources perhaps. Employee's basic assumptions contribute greatly to an organization's culture. Much time, experience and study would be required to truly investigate and understand the deep and multifaceted impact basic assumptions have on organizational culture. Unfortunately, a three month study of the culture of an investigated company, as in this case, simply does not provide enough time to research this topic in the required depth and would require a long-term study to be carried out on its own merits.

Whilst evaluating the questionnaires from the survey carried out in the aforementioned organization, it became apparent that competitive thinking was once very characteristic amongst the company's employees. However, after the company started to get into a problematic phase, people tended to be less competitive and more supportive of each other.[1] Based on that understanding, it would seem that competitiveness was a strategy of action that worked as long as the company was successful. In times of crisis, when the environment became unpredictable, it was therefore observed that employee strategy adapted to suit the circumstances.

Deal and Kennedy's cultural model

In their book *Corporate cultures: the rites and rituals of corporate life*, Deal and Kennedy (1982) characterize four different types of organizational culture, each based upon a degree of feedback and reward, as well as a willingness to take risks. Deal and Kennedy are of the opinion that organizational culture is one of the most important drivers of success.

The first important element of organizational culture is the feedback and specific rewards organizational mem-

[1] cf. App. B.

bers receive which inform them as to how well they are doing their job. According to Deal and Kennedy, short-term feedback is essential to creating a consistent culture. The reason is that feedback corrects ineffective behavior and if people refuse to learn to change they will eventually be fired. On the other hand, long-term feedback gives people a long-range view into the future indeed yet bad behavior may go uncorrected in the short-term.

The second dimension Deal and Kennedy focus on is risk. Most people do not like uncertainty or risk and try to avoid it whilst others develop their full potential in uncertain situations. These two groups of people need to be motivated in different ways to manage risk and uncertainty. Low risk is usually accepted to a certain point, whilst high risk must either be accepted or it will have to be managed. The four culture types are described as follows (p.107):

Work-hard, play-hard culture

In the work-hard, play-hard culture (rapid reward and low risk), there is scarcely stress due to uncertainty. Stress rather comes from quantity of work. The high speed action in that culture leads to quick reactions. This culture will often be found in software companies and restaurants.

Tough-guy macho culture

In the tough-guy macho culture (rapid feedback and high risk); stress is caused by the high risk and the probable loss or gain of reward. People rather focus on the present than the long-term future. Typical representatives of such culture are found for example in police, surgeons and sports.

Process culture

In the process culture (slow feedback and low risk) bureaucracy can emerge as a means of maintaining the status quo. There is hardly any stress except that created internally through politics and witlessness of the organization. The focus of such a culture is on past and future security. It is typically found in banks and insurance companies.

Bet-the-company culture

In the bet-the-company culture (slow feedback and high risk) the high risk causes stress. Although the long-term view is a given, slow feedback is another stress factor because much energy is put into safeguarding that things go as planned People get to know the outcome of their actions with delay. Examples of these cultures are found in oil companies and aircraft manufacturers.

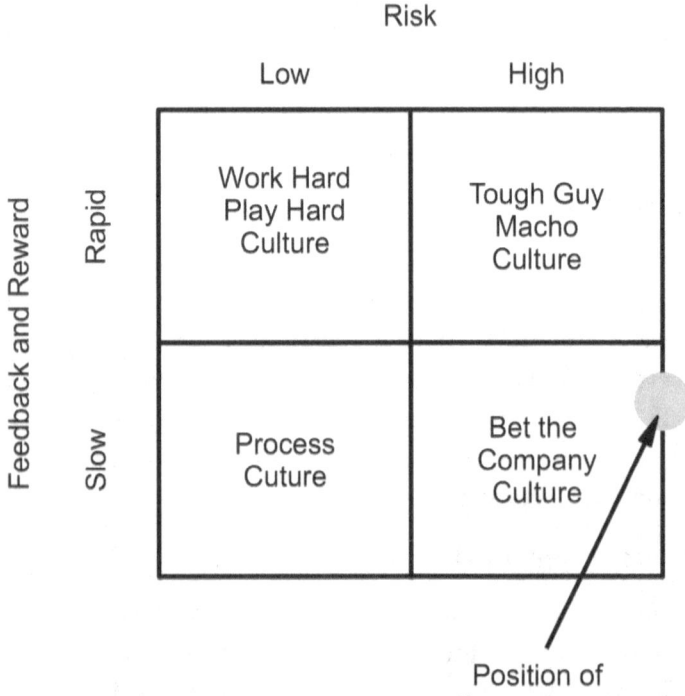

Fig. 2: *Culture model of Deal and Kennedy (Based on Deal and Kennedy (1982) p. 108)*.

By trying to assign the investigated company's culture to Deal and Kennedy's model, it became quite clear that different cultural characteristics for different departments exist, depending on the type of work people do. Overall, the company's culture most closely resembled a *Process Culture*. Feedback was rather slow because the process of developing and selling a machine is very long and can take even a number of years. The results of daily decision-making often do not become visible until a long time after they have been made. There are also situations in the company when feedback is given extremely fast. For example, when a technician fits an incorrect part into a machine it soon will be noticed.

In the past, the company had monthly feedback questionnaires. These were discontinued when it was discovered that they were more of a bothersome routine that rarely resulted in improvements. An inherent problem with creating improvements is that it requires change, which may be seen as a threat since it is human nature to try to keep all things stable. Such conservatism might have been another reason for the abolishment of the feedback questionnaires. In this company, risk was rather low, mainly because the company operates on a known territory. Existing models of machine are developed incrementally and not many new, innovative products are created. The company is better known for its offering of established machine technology of the highest quality in its field rather than for its innovation.

Coherence of national culture and organizational culture

Hofstede (1984) surveyed aspects of national cultures in different parts of the world and identified five dimensions of culture which can also be found in organizations.

Power-distance

National cultures with a high power-distance have, according to Hofstede's survey, high inequalities, whereas in cultures with low power-distance there is the effort to minimize such inequalities. Within organizations with a high power-distance the organization's members expect power to be distributed unequally, and also accept this fact (p.65-66).

In comparison to ten other countries from around the world, power-distance in the cultures of German organizations is quite low, according to Hofstede's power-distance index. (Germany: 35 points, Mexico (highest) 81 points) (p. 79).

In keeping with this low German power-distance average, the investigated company's power-distance level was also rather low and its power structure demonstrates a fair amount of equality. A great deal of information is provided from the executive to all employees at all hierarchical levels because the company sees its strength in the knowledge of its employees. Employees know their managers very well and are able to estimate their behavior. Managers there are very much open to criticism. The company encourages its employees to voice fair criticism, independent from their own or the criticized person's hierarchical position. Power distance grew during the crises, because decisions had to be made quickly and sharing details of each and every decision was seen as more counterproductive than productive. Information was, nevertheless, regularly provided from managerial heads to all employees. At the same time, speculation about several scenarios could not be avoided.

Uncertainty-avoidance: In uncertainty-avoiding cultures members fear uncertain and unknown situations and therefore try to avoid them. These people like to be busy, precise and punctual, whereas in low uncertainty-avoidance cultures, aspects like punctuality and precision are less important (p.110).

The occurrence of uncertainty-avoidance at the company varied depending on the department people were working in and the job they were doing. However, most departments tended to have a low uncertainty-avoidance culture. Although precision is very important in all departments, room for creative action and independent decision making exists since not every activity is subject to tough regulations.

Individualism—collectivism: In an individualistic society, a person is more focused on his or her own welfare over that of the group as a whole. In a collectivistic society the contrary is the norm, as the welfare of the group is given higher priority and people tend to care more about each other's wellbeing. However, this does not necessarily mean that individualism is incompatible with collectivism (p.184-187).

In the company in question, it could be observed that the culture is individualistic as well as collectivistic but collectivism had a greater impact. When people or departments became too egoistic and their behavior had a noticeable, negative impact on others, they would receive quick feedback to change this behavior. People are seen as individuals who contribute to the function of the whole and the welfare of the company has the highest priority. Collectivism was also seen to be represented in the cooperative management style which could not exist to such an extent if the interest of individual persons was the most important criteria.

Masculinity — femininity

Masculinity indicates the extent to which gender roles are distinct and accepted in society. In high femininity societies gender does not play an important role and the roles of males and females overlap, as do their attributes (p.176).

In our investigated organization, the German average level of femininity was seen to exist, albeit at a rather low level. As with most German institutions, there were fewer women in executive positions and none at the highest levels of management. However the organizational culture encouraged appropriate respect towards women and ensured that women were regarded by their male colleagues as equals.

Long-term orientation — short-term orientation

Short-term oriented cultures focus more on quick results and reciprocation whereas long-term oriented cultures stress perseverance and thrift (p.160-162).

This company has a rather long-term orientation, an attribute that is dictated by its product. As stated before, the development and selling of a specialist machine takes quite a long time. These machines also operate for many years which means that spare parts and service must be concurrently provided for machines that were sold even ten years earlier. Of course, whilst there are also short-term factors that the company has to consider, the long-term issues are given more priority. An exception occurred during the financial crisis. During that difficult time, every short-term event had great importance and the focus on long-term goals was pushed somewhat into the background even if never completely forgotten.

The ecological and social need for cultural change

Lyberth (2008) talks about the suicidal tendencies of society due to its fixation on *one truth*[1]. These suicidal tendencies of modern society can also be looked upon from the aspect of the traditional method of conflict-solving through combat with an enemy. Gillett (1963) refers to Arnold Toynbee's twelve volumes of *A Study of History*, in which Toynbee analyzes the rise and fall of civilizations. In this context, he uses the term *Suicidal-ness of Militarism* (p.8). Even today, this suicidal-ness not only of militarism but also of whole societies can be observed. Most great nations keep building stock piles of arms, even though nonviolent alternatives have been shown as effective means for resolving conflicts. Mankind also seems to be fighting 'World War III against nature', therefore sawing at its own branch of the tree which gives it life. For example, the American State fears and fights terrorism whilst it takes less action to stop climate change, even with the knowledge that according to a study by Kofi A. Annan of Ghana, the seventh Secretary-General of The United Nations, there are some 300,000 people dying each year as a result of climate change (Bolzen, 2009, p. 1). In contrast, according to the US Min-

---

1 cf. the chapter Culture page 13 above.

istry of Foreign Affairs, there were some 20,000 people killed by terrorist attacks in the year 2006 worldwide (Festl, 2007, p.1). The suicidal program of violence against nature is active and evident. Rainforests are being cleared, fossil energy resources grow scarce, and environmental pollution increases whilst the world population grows by 80 Million people each year. Today there are almost a billion people suffering from hunger (Lindemann and Heim, 2010, p. 11). There is an endless list of cases that show that civilization is more likely to perish by suicide than murder. On top of this, surveys show that people are becoming less satisfied, even though physical wealth has increased in the last centuries. Likewise, the gap between the rich and poor constantly widens (Theobald, 2009, p. 165). Increasing aggression and violence among young people is becoming a growing problem for societies (Behrend, 2006, p. 1). An increased loss of identity amongst teenagers contributes greatly to violence and extremism (Being (2010) p. 1). These are only a few examples yet they illustrate well the immense need for a consciousness of the common social responsibility carried jointly by economic organizations, according to Lindemann and Heim (2010), p. 11). Of course, governments carry responsibilities and the ability to create change too, yet at the organizational level there is a great deal which the 'average citizen' can do to create change, as will be described later.[1]

---

1 cf. The link between culture in organizations and societies on page 32

The economic need for cultural change

Not only has the worldwide economic crises clearly illustrated that the money-driven culture of Western societies needs to change dramatically, but there are indications that organizations of all types need to change their cultures fundamentally as well. One very clear example of this need is the general unproductiveness of employees. According to a 2008 *Gallup Survey on the Engagement Index of Employees*, nearly 90 percent of German employees do not feel committed to the company they work for.

The performance of a company is very much dependent upon the stand-by-duty of its employees. This means that having loyal and highly motivated employees with a high emotional engagement with their company is the source of a strong competitive advantage (Kleine, 2009, p. 1). With this in mind, high, little and low emotional engagement are defined according to the above article (ibid., 2009) as follows:

High emotional engagement:

Employees with a high emotional engagement are loyal, productive and are rarely absent. Companies with these types of employees benefit from their consistent performance and attendance.

Little emotional engagement:

Employees with less emotional engagement feel only limitedly bound to their place of employment. They are still productive, but tend to do only the amount of work asked of them and nothing more. They have more days absent and a less consistent level of performance.

No emotional engagement:

Employees with no emotional engagement are present only physically, not mentally. They are unhappy with their workplace situation, have many days absent and even work against the interests of their company. Their performance is highly inconsistent, and often these employees have already carried out their inner denunciation for the company while they are still in its employ.

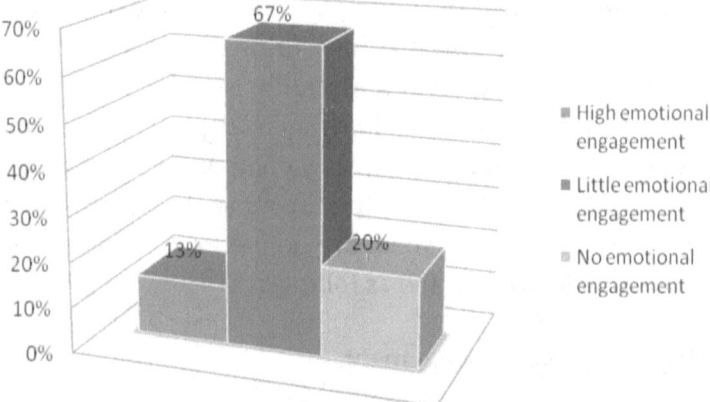

Fig. 3: Engagement Index in Germany 2008 (Based on Kleine (2009) p. 1.)

According to Marco Nink, Strategic Consultant for Gallup Germany, the percentage of highly emotionally engaged German employees is only in the low middle-field compared with employees from other countries like Great Britain (20 %) or USA (29%). Employees with low emotional engagement are absent two more days than their colleagues with high emotional engagement, and employees with no emotional engagement are absent an additional four more days.

According to the evaluation of the Gallup poll, the economic costs to a company of low and no emotional engagement employees can be between 81 and 109 million Euros per year (Kleine, 2009, p. 2).

The Engagement Index at the Investigated Company

The following graphic shows the engagement index at the company investigated according to the evaluation of a survey made by the researcher. It does not necessarily represent the whole company because the return rate of questionnaires was only about 50%. But at least nearly 50% of employees affirmed that they were highly emotionally engaged according to the above definitions.[1]

Reasons for low/no emotional engagement and approach

According to Nink, the level of emotional engagement is very much linked with an employee's direct manager. Many employees criticized that they did not get enough appreciation or that their opinion went unheard within the company. On top of that, many employees were of the opinion that they worked in positions for which they were not really suited. Not even the financial crisis lead to more engagement of employees which would indicate that the fear of job loss is not effective in motivating em-

1 cf. App. B.

ployees. The major reason why employees give notice is because of their boss so it is therefore important for companies to improve their management personnel at all levels within the organization (cf. Kleine, 2009, p. 2). Assuming that Nink is right and emotional engagement is very much linked to an employee's direct leader, people at the investigated company were generally very content with their leaders. This assumption is supported by the result of Survey 1 on the issue of trust. Most people believed that they had a trustworthy relationship with their managers.[1] There is more information on the topic of trust in the section on Nonviolent communication based on Marshall Rosenberg on page 107 ff.

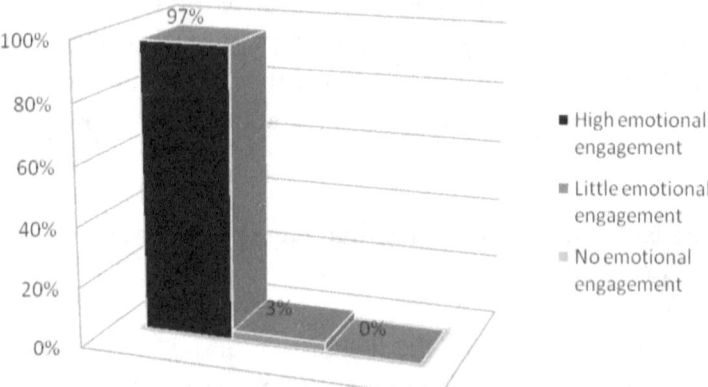

Fig. 4: Engagement Index of the Investigated Company. Survey 1, App. B.

Global Productivity Study

Proudfoot Consulting published a global productivity study in 2002[2] in which the result stated that only an av-

---

1 cf. App. B.
2 The study comprised 1,357 individual studies from

erage 59% of optimum capacity was being used in the surveyed companies. Germany was seen as being the most productive at 63%. This study also found poor management to be the main cause of lost productivity (Proudfoot Consulting, 2002, p. 9).

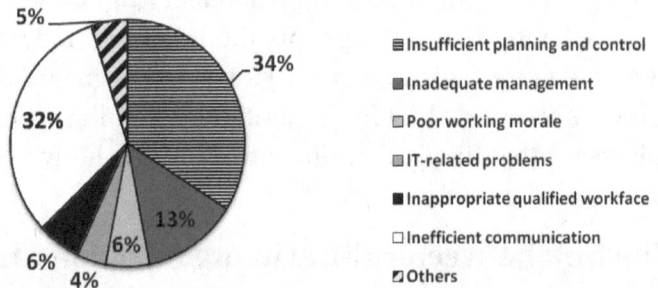

Fig. 5: Productivity study 2002: Reasons for productivity loss in organizations worldwide (Based on Proudfoot consulting (2002) p. 9.)

According to Nink, corporate leaders need to understand their own strengths and weaknesses to be able to realize how others see their management style. An anonymous survey within a company can help to provide more insights. Then, it is possible to improve the degree of emotional engagement (cf. Kleine, 2009, p. 2).

According to employee opinion the greatest productivity loss at the company in question was caused by insufficient planning and control, as well as inefficient communication.

companies in seven countries: Australia, Austria, France, Germany, South Africa, United Kingdom and the United States.

Evidence for the necessity for economic improvements reaches beyond individual businesses to include, for example, the increasing national debt. However, the focus of this work is on organizations and their impact on society will be examined in the next chapter. Senge criticizes the use of fragmentation when focusing on organizations saying that it fragments the issue and risks the loss of a more holistic review. However, fragmentation can be a necessary tool for accurately examining specific sub-issues that finally contribute to a more cohesive presentation of the entire topic.

The link between culture in organizations and societies

The IGOS (Individual, Group/Team, Organization, and Society) model (Engelking, 2012, p.39) is a visual model created to illustrate the influence of organizations upon the societies within which they are situated. The model shows that society and organizations exert influence over each other and that even an individual in an organization can influence the society indirectly.

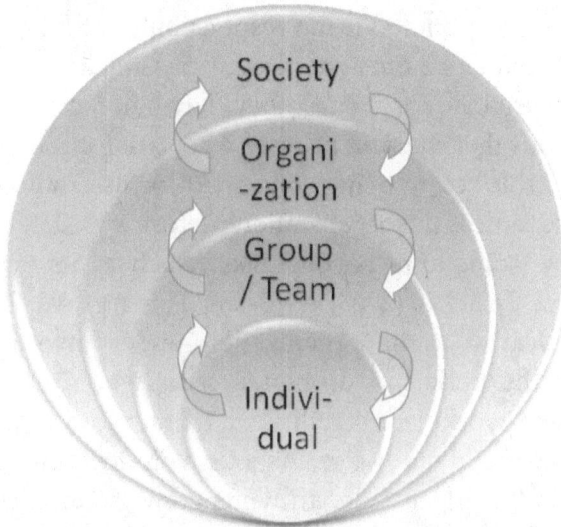

Fig. 6: The IGOS. Adapted from Engelking (2012, p.39).

In the chapters above various points have been made regarding the reasons why cultural changes in society are crucial. Nevertheless, a discussion about the necessity of that task having to fall to organizations is still required. Accordingly, Senge (1990) quoted Edward Simon, president of Hermann Miller: "Business is the only institution that has a chance, [...] to fundamentally improve the injustice that exists in the world."(p.5) Drucker points out that creating a healthy society is in the best interests for an organization because a healthy organization can hardly survive within a sick environment. Drucker also indicated that problems are not solved by looking the other way when they only disappear from one's range of vision. Problems disappear when someone works to correct them. Drucker asks yet another question about the responsibility of business in society, namely as to what extent organizations should be accountable for issues they have not created. He points out that the first priority is to care for the organization itself before being concerned for its environment because, unless the organization performs well, it cannot improve something beyond itself, such as its environment (cf. Drucker (2003) p. 57-58). This fact was shown quite clearly in the organization under investigation during the period of economic crisis when its performance on workplace stability was rather low and many people were given notice. As jobs were lost, the atmosphere in the affected departments grew gloomy because during the crisis many companies found themselves in a similar situation and whole societies were being negatively affected. Through unstable performance the organization was also making a negative contribution to its local environment whereas the opposite had been the case during the good times.

The difference between culture and structure

According to Schein, visible structure is part of organizational culture[1]. Fritz (1996) points out that organizational structure is not something static, but something essential for creating stability. It must therefore contain various dynamic relationships that create balance, strength, and solidity within an organization. Fritz defines structure as, "an entity formed by the influence individual parts have on each other and on the whole" (p. 16). This definition includes three important aspects:

1 cf. page 14.

First, structure consists of individual elements, yet these elements exist in interaction. Secondly, the interacting parts form the totality of the structure. (This is important to remember because people tend to think of parts as isolated elements). Thirdly, many individual factors influence the structure (cf. Frith, 1996, p. 16).

Many organizations use charts that illustrate the organization's hierarchy to display what they understand as structure. Like Fritz, Senge (1990) states that systemic structure arises from interrelationships, not between people but between other important variables that influence people's behavior, such as an engineer's products, ideas or managerial know-how (cf. p. 44). This is an important difference compared with organizational culture, a view of which is much broader including, for example, relationships between people and an understanding of their basic values. Just as with culture, structure also influences people's behavior. Structure can be designed more easily than culture but it has a considerable impact on culture. Thus by creating a structure that advances nonviolent behavior, components of a nonviolent culture can already be formed.

Structures at the investigated company developed from such organizational values as openness to criticism and from the flat hierarchies. These structures enabled department management to take part in decision-making through consultancy with top management which considered their advice in their decision-making processes.

The exertion of influence on organizational culture

According to Hofstede (1984), national cultures consist of their people's *mental programs*, which are created in families during early childhood. Those programs develop further in schools and organizations. The disparity between different cultures is mainly expressed in the values of their people (p.11). This idea leads to Hofstede's definition of culture as "collective programming of the mind" (p.13). This suggests that:

1. The minds of people in a culture can be programmed, and due to the programming the culture can be changed.
2. Values play an important role in a culture.

Schein (1995) too, is of the opinion that organizational cultures can be influenced. As mentioned above, the founder of the organization, or later its leader, can have great influence upon that organization's culture. According to Schein, a leader is confronted with the task of understanding the culture of the group he leads. By creating a group or an organization, the leader automatically creates its culture as at the same time.

Already existing cultures, on the contrary, affect the criteria of organizational leadership and therefore dictate who may assume a leading position (p.29). This is an important example of why it is necessary for a leader of an organization to truly understand its culture. Also, a leader must be able to influence change within an exist-

Culture

ing culture wherever necessary. If a leader, for example, realizes that the organization insists upon applying obviously inefficient work methods that could even endanger its survival, this leader must have enough influence to create positive changes (p.19). Another challenge to the leaders of existing organizations is that different groups within large organizations can have multifarious cultures and therefore act according to their individual goals and not necessarily for the welfare of the organization as a whole. Thus an important task of a leader is the creation or even re-creation of organizational culture (p.20), to enable greater efficiency. Schein's opinion of managing culture as one of the leader's main tasks contains the assumption that culture can be influenced by leaders.

Contrary to this, Frost (1985) is of the opinion that organizational culture is hardly capable of management. He states that cultures are created unconsciously and therefore are difficult to predict or control and the effort to manage them is unlikely to be rewarded (p.156). In his definition, Frost compares organizational culture with a "bubble of meaning covering the world,"(Frost, 1991, p.287) created by the humans who live within it. Frost states that while people create culture, they can hardly influence it because, for the most part, it is created unconsciously. However, there are several known methods by which the unconscious can be consciously influenced, such as through *Autogenic Training*, acting as an ideal, training mental models, and other methods.

According to Deal and Kennedy (1982), the greatest influence upon an organization's culture is its social and economic environment. Yet they also state that organizational culture can be shaped to conform to the society within which it exists (p.13). As pictured in the IGOS-model above, the environment does not only have influence upon the organizational culture but the inverse is also true.

Therefore, we dare to conclude that the advocators' assumption which states that management or leadership can influence organizational cultures is correct. Because management and leadership are the facets that have the most influence over organizations, our discussion will concentrate mostly on leadership and its impact on cultural development.

In latter times, personal changes in leadership at the organization we were investigating were slowly leading to noticeable cultural changes. This seemed to underpin the statement that management and leadership have a great influence on culture. These cultural changes had not been introduced consciously and therefore had not been guided in a particular direction, having simply arisen from the various leadership styles and ways of leading.

Aspects of culture in the investigated organization

As the company in question now had to struggle for its survival during the worldwide economic crisis which hit the engineering branch generally very hard with its high

Culture

proportion of exports, top management at the company had to take command and could not afford to spend time considering culture issues. Whilst top management was busy with other concerns, second tier management tried to support the existing culture with targeted action. However, according to internal information, no one had ever left the company due to issues with its culture. This fact proves the existence of an employee-friendly culture within the organization and is proof that the crisis could hardly have emerged from a weak or poor culture. Nevertheless a lot of potential for improvement remains, as with all organizations.

Violence vs. Nonviolence

Definitions of violence

Violence according to Englander (2003) is "aggressive behavior with the intent to cause harm (physical or psychological)" (p. 3). In her definition, Englander points out the importance of the word *intent* because physical or psychological harm inflicted without intent is not considered to be violence.

Warshaw (1998) quotes several definitions of violence. It becomes clear that there is no single, cohesive definition of violence. Warshaw makes the criticism that many definitions focus on physical harm whilst at the same time neglecting to recognize psychological violence. Warshaw examines violence in the workplace and quotes the definition of work-related violence from the UK Health and Safety Executive (HSE) as, "any incident, in which an employee is abused, threatened or assaulted by a member of the public in circumstances arising out of the course of his or her employment. Assailants may be patients, clients or co-workers." This definition is very broad and includes all kinds of harm or discomfort, even by an innocent bystander, inflicted upon a person in the workplace. In this context, Warshaw criticizes the lack of information and literature aimed at preventing violence in the workplace (ch. 51.2).

According to Gandhi, violence is something that corrupts and degrades humans. It meets hatred with hatred and therefore promotes man's degradation. He is of the opinion that violence will eliminate men if it takes hold of the mind of a great mass (cf. Gandhi, Merton and Kurlansky (2007) p. 35-43).

Causes of violence

Holler (2005) sees occurrences of violence as a result of problems. According to her, a problem can lead to a conflict. Problems as well as conflicts can lead to violence. These terms are defined as follows:

Problem: an actual need that is not followed or does not perform itself.

Conflict: two actual needs that seem to be incompatible.

Violence: needs enforced without respect for the needs

of others, or the attempt to punish other humans (p. 23).[1]

Gandhi believes all violence arises from seven instances (cf. Gandhi, 1998, p. 90), which are also known the *Seven Deadly Sins*:

1. Wealth without work
2. Pleasure without conscience
3. Knowledge without character
4. Commerce without morality
5. Science without humanity
6. Worship without sacrifice
7. Politics without principle

Each of these seven forms of behavior can, to a greater or lesser extent, influence all types of organizations whilst they all interact with each other. The following examples demonstrate how these *Deadly Sins* can lead to violence and harm.

1. Wealth without work

People's desire to become rich without having to work was a major factor leading to the worldwide economic crisis. The desire for higher and higher interest rates on money, together with risky speculation, lead to the

---

[1] Translation, original German version of the definitions: *Problem: Ein aktuelles Bedürfnis wird nicht berücksichtigt oder erfüllt sich nicht. Konflikt: Zwei aktuelle Bedürfnisse stehen sich scheinbar unvereinbar gegenüber. Gewalt: Bedürfnisse werden ohne Rücksicht auf die Bedürfnisse anderer durchgesetzt. / Der versuch, andere Menschen zu bestrafen.*

collapse of some major financial institutions and finally to the worldwide financial and economic crisis.[1]

2. Pleasure without conscience

A very devastating example of pleasure without conscience is the sexual abuse of children along with abuse in general for the sake of a moment's enjoyment at the cost of others. This is often at the cost of the weaker and less protected members of society.

3. Knowledge without character

An excellent example of knowledge without character is the creation and use of the nuclear bomb. In an organization it is often expressed in the form of expert power, where superior access to information is used to gain personal advantage.

4. Commerce without morality

Commerce without morality has become a larger problem since globalization. Low-wage countries try to compete, despite extremely poor pay, by using child labour and the exploitation of their people whilst consumers in western countries happily go on bargain hunting without caring why shops can offer their products at such low prices.

5. Science without humanity

A cruel aspect of science without humanity is animal experimentation, especially those that do not serve the

---

[1] http://www.finanzkrise-2008.de, accessed 11.05.2010.

welfare of humans but are carried out only for the sake of knowledge.

6. Worship without sacrifice

Extremism and terrorism are examples of worship without sacrifice as is lip-service to religion without acts of compassion.

7. Politics without principle

All kinds of violations of human rights in conjunction with politics are examples of politics without principle. In the same way political corruption and personal advantage fit to this.

In Survey 3, carried out as part of this investigation, far the greatest agreement was reached on Gandhi's statement *commerce without morality*. 70% of those asked totally agreed that this point leads to violence and 60% totally agreed that they tried to avoid commerce without morality in their lives.[1]

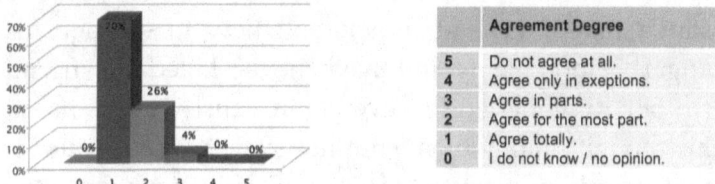

Fig. 7: *Degree of agreement that commerce without morality leads to violence. Survey 3, app. D.*

This result of the survey demonstrates the awareness of this problem. Companies that act morally have a real

---

1 For more opinions on the seven deadly sins see appendix D.

Unique Selling Proposition (USP). At this point, companies must not fall into the trap of using morals as selling tools. The focus must be on the welfare of its contemporaries. Wolfgang Mewes, developer of the EKS-method[1] states that in the long term those companies whose highest priority is to advance the interests of all are the most successful. Many examples support his thesis and numerous companies use the principles of EKS developed by Mewes (cf. Bußmann, 2010, p. 39-40).

Rosenberg (2009) observes the subject of violence from a different point of view, one that agrees with Gandhi's beliefs. According to Rosenberg, violence occurs from the assumption that other people are responsible for one's pain and therefore deserve punishment. Rosenberg tells of an experience with a man in prison for murdering his friend during a fight. He taught the prisoner about the different ways anger occurs and erupts into violence, about being responsible for one's emotions and about nonviolent communication. After having absorbed the points of Rosenberg's lessons, this prisoner stated that if he had understood how to manage his anger before, he would have never killed his friend (p.168). Rosenberg offers even more causes of violence in his model of nonviolent communication. A key cause is that people in western societies usually learn from the very beginning to be judgmental of everything. This judging creates not only anger that can lead to violence but, Rosenberg believes, is violence itself. People also

1   EKS = *Engpasskonzentrierten Verhaltens- und Führungsstrategie* (shortage-oriented behavior and leading strategy)

tend to be self-critical due to actions that their parents, society, or even they themselves deem to be wrong or bad (p.149-150). Gandhi (2003) agrees with Rosenberg. He is of the opinion that judging everything as right or wrong leads to violence because people tend to fight against what they perceive as being 'wrong'. (cf. p.23). The ancient Sioux (Native American people) knew about the negative potential of judgement. They recited the prayer, "Dear Great Spirit, keep me from criticizing and judging someone else, before I have not worn his moccasins for two weeks"(Carnegie, 1999, p.150)[1].

Judgements work mainly on the basis of so-called static language. The psychologist O. J. Harvey studied the coherence between static language and violence in different cultures of the world. His results showed that there is a high correlation between static language and violence (cf. Rosenberg, 2009, p.21). When trying to use non-violent communication, the author realized that the German language is full of judging, labeling, analyzing, and diagnosing terminology.[2] In the survey concerning non-violent communication, people's opinions varied greatly on the question of whether the German language is violent. Four people did not agree at all whereas three people totally agreed.[3]

---

1 Translation, original quotation: *O großer Geist, bewahre mich davor, jemand zu kritisieren und zu verurteilen, ehe ich nicht zwei Wochen seine Mokassins getragen habe.*
2 cf. App. G.
3 cf. App. E.

Whilst Gandhi's *Deadly Sins*, should be avoided to prevent violence, the mere avoidance of violence is not yet nonviolence. The definition of nonviolence shaped by Mahatma Gandhi goes beyond avoidance. In the chapter *A definition of nonviolence based on Gandhi's thinking*, below, Gandhi's explanation of nonviolence will be discussed in more depth.

Violence against animals and the environment

Mahatma Gandhi taught his grandson Arun not only about violence against humans, but also against nature. Once, Arun threw away a little piece of pencil hoping to get a new one from his grandfather. Instead of giving Arun a new pencil, Mahatma ordered Arun in the middle of the night to find the old piece. When Arun finally came back with the piece, Mahatma told him that throwing things away that were still useful was violence against nature. This story illustrates Gandhi's belief that if every human threw away useful items, enormous resources would be lost, and by depleting the Earth's resources, people create imbalance in the world. Gandhi states that especially rich people tend to waste resources because they can buy whatever they wish. The increasing imbalance between rich and poor promotes negative attitudes towards others along with violence and crime, demonstrating how violence against nature and against men interacts. Mahatma Gandhi sums up this theory by saying, "The earth can produce enough for everyone's needs, but not for everyone's greed." Waste in wealthy countries enforces poverty in poor countries, which Gandhi considers as violence against humanity.

Gandhi also taught his grandson not to use violence against animals. Gandhi was a vegetarian due to his belief that no creature must be done harm to or be killed by humans (cf. Gandhi, 2003, p.101-109).

The role of organizations concerning violence against nature is quite apparent today. Organizations must use resources wisely, rely more upon sustainable energy and recognize that they are not only part of nature but also dependent on it. Alt (2007) states, that nature does not need humans, it is humans who need nature to survive. Alt also underlines the power of consumers, whether they are private or organizational consumers. Those who support, for example, environmentally friendly or nonviolent energy producers will drive more energy leaders towards the production of these types of energy sources (p.197).

At the firm in question, the only real environmentally protective action being taken was that customers were being made aware of the possibility of using biodegradable materials on their machines. Innate environmental protection measures are the durability of the machines and their secure operation. These measures help to save resources but this aspect is only a side effect of customer's machine requirements.

The destructive effect of violence in organizations

Warshaw (1998) quotes a statement of Unison[1] in a

1 Unison is the "British union of health care and

newsletter 1992. According to Unison, violence is the most threatening risk employees face at their workplace and which very often leads to harm. Violence can lead to extreme occupational stress and injures a person's self-esteem. It can even lead to the inability of continuing in the job (ch. 51.2).

The following story which Zittlau (2003) tells, demonstrates the destructiveness of violence in management, even in a case that would appear to be harmless at first sight. A woman called Katja worked in an advertising agency. She was working on an extensive project. For its termination she either needed support or a more realistic dead-line. Being a self-confident woman, she went to talk to her boss to discuss the problem. Right away the boss showed what so often is called *understanding* by saying: "I really know how much you would like to be at home with your family but even though you are missed there, your family will be happy and proud of you when you come home with the promotion we are considering for you." Katja did not get the necessary support she had sought, nor was she given a more realistic deadline. Instead, she merely got *understanding* with the hint of a promotion. Slowly, she began to realize that what her boss displayed was not understanding at all but in fact he had been putting her under pressure. If she wanted to get the promotion, she would need to have made the unrealistic expectation placed upon her somehow realistic. Alternatively, if she preferred her family to her job, then her boss inferred that she could go home

governmental service workers."

and stay there. That woman became a victim of emotional violence. In a society that forswears physical violence as far as possible, there is still an apparent inability to recognize and disapprove of emotional violence.

The outcome of violence in the story of Katja is that she developed self-doubt after the conversation with her boss. Instead of the support she wished to receive, she was left with the feeling that she possibly neglects her family, an impression she had not thought of previously. Secondly, she felt even more under pressure to finish the project within the given deadline if she wanted to get the promised promotion. Katja can either claim the promotion or determine it as a threat. This awareness might restrict her actual productivity for the company.

Because of the emotional violence inflicted upon Katja, she does not know what she could have achieved if she had been given the support which she had sought. Therefore she did not recognize her full potential nor will she. This case can be compared with a tulip: when looking at only the bulb, no one can know exactly what it will look like unless it receives the resources necessary for growth and no one will ever know the truth of its full potential. By inflicting violence upon that tulip by covering it with concrete its beauty will never be known. This picture of the tulip demonstrates how violence destroys truth (cf. p.65-68).

Violence in language

In an example by Lindemann and Heim (2010), similar to the story of Katja, an employee goes to his boss to tell him that he cannot finish his record by midday as requested (p.32-33).

The following table shows possibilities for the boss to answer in a violent way.

	Dominance Strategies	Possible answers	Violence because...
1	To command, order, ask, expect, demand, require	"I expect you to deliver the record by midday!"	The boss overrides employee. First, he tries to push him into a certain direction without seeking a full picture of the situation. Then he shows that he does not know how to do something. With the use of diagnosis and judgments the boss tells the employee, that there is something wrong with him.
2	To threaten, alert, either…or strategies	"If you do not deliver the record until midday, I will…"	
3	To moralize, preach	"Reliably employees inform early, when they cannot meet the deadline."	
4	To give advices, give hasty solutions	"I have always told you to prioritize."	
5	To give lectures, disabuse, give facts	"You know we need the record for…"	
6	To reproach, judge, criticize judgmentally	"You are so unreliable."	
7	To praise, adulate	"You always get things right. You will manage it by midday, won't you?"	
8	To insult, make somebody look silly	"Everyone has to wait for your record, now – how awkward!"	

	Dominance Strategies	Possible answers	Violence because...
9	To interpret, make a diagnosis, analyze	"It seems you are overextended. As a graduate I would start this in a different way!"	
10	I have the feeling, that-sentences	"I have the feeling that you cannot cope with the task."	
11	To assign blame	"Because of you, the whole project will be delayed."	
12	To console, to evince sympathy, spare	"You poor sop. Now everything depends on you — must be quite a burden."	
13	To study, ask, interrogate, why-questions	"Why do you tell me only now?"	The employee gets nowhere or gets told, that he made something wrong.
14	Bossiness	"It is your duty to deliver this record in time."	The boss yields his responsibility or seizes it so much that all equality is lost.

Table 1: Examples of dominance strategies in language (Lindemann and Heim. 2010, p. 32-33.)

This 'harmless' example was used to give a first impression of what violence in language can look like. Very often during everyday (conflict) situations, language is used as an instrument of power to get what one wants, even at the expense of others (cf. Lindemann and Heim, 2010, p.11), thus creating frustration, aggression and violence.

In the survey carried out here on dominance strategies, the examples 4, 5, 7, and 13 were experienced and used by about half of the questioned people. Examples 2 and 8 were only experienced and used by 4% (example 2) and 7% (example 8) of the polled people. Examples 2 and 8 are more obvious dominance strategies than examples 4, 5, 7 and 13.[1] This shows that violence in society today is covert. Very often it is subtle and therefore hard to detect.

	Dominance Strategies	I experience this strategy regularly (several times a week)	I use this strategy myself.
2	To threaten, alert, either…or strategies	4%	4%
4	To give advices, give hasty solutions	48%	37%
5	To give lectures, disabuse, give facts	48%	48%
7	To praise, adulate	22%	48%
8	To insult, make somebody look silly	7%	7%
13	To study, ask, interrogate, why-questions	48%	52%

Table 2: Evaluation of dominance strategies in language cf. Survey 3, app. D.

Mahatma Gandhi was of the opinion that such passive or emotional violence is more insidious than obvious physical violence. Passive violence is very often hidden but creates a lot of anger and hatred and can therefore become the very source of active physical violence. Gandhi compares passive violence with an oil pipeline.

1 cf. App. D.

He asks how to put out a fire when the pipeline that ignited the inferno is not capped. Gandhi argues that all efforts for peace and nonviolence will fail as long as the 'pipeline' remains active.[1] Therefore, the whole chapter entitled *Nonviolent communication based on Marshall Rosenberg* on page 107 deals with the important issue of nonviolent communication.

A definition of nonviolence based on Gandhi's thinking

The term nonviolence was very much shaped by Mahatma Gandhi therefore this definition will be based on his understanding of nonviolence. According to Zittlau (2003), Gandhi called his way of life *Ahimsa*. The word *Ahimsa* arises from the Indian word *himsa*, meaning hurt, harm or abuse. The Indian prefix *A* shows the negation of a word. Thus *Ahimsa* can be translated as *free of abusiveness*, or *nonviolence* (p.63).

Gandhi et al. (2007)point out the inseparability of nonviolence and love. He calls nonviolent acts that are motivated by love "nonviolence of the strong" whereas "nonviolence of the weak" is used to describe a policy that tries to harm an enemy and lacks a loving motive. For true nonviolence, one is ready to sacrifice everything; it is the highest form of bravery and fully lovedriven. Nonviolence presupposes humility (cf. p. 49-50).

According to Gandhi (2003), nonviolence is based on these five elements:

---

1   cf. Foreword by Gandhi in: Rosenberg (2009) p. 9-10.

- Love
- Appreciation
- Understanding
- Respect
- Acceptance

The authors have come up with the acronym **LAURA** based on the initial letters, to help as a reminder.

Gandhi states that nonviolence is not to be used as a formula and different methods might be required contingently. By the use of violent solutions, fixed actions for certain happenings are often institutionalized (p. 122). This might be one reason for the wide spread use of violence in Western society. Nonviolence requires innovation and unique reactions according to the given circumstances and therefore continuous learning. This very aspect at the same time also offers great opportunities and the possibilities of nonviolence are unlimited (ibid.).

One of Gandhi's basic beliefs came from the Hindu principle that there is good and bad in every human being. By appealing to bad qualities, conflict and violence occur. On the contrary, the result of appealing to good qualities is compassion and understanding (p. 127). Zittlau (2003) writes about trust – a foundational element of nonviolence. Gandhi was often confronted with the reproach that he trusted people too much. But Gandhi stated that he would rather be betrayed a hundred times than be suspecting of his opponent. Zittlau calls

Gandhi's deep trust in men "the only productive strategy"(p. 123). He brings forward the argument that by trusting someone that person can prove whether he deserved the trust or not. Depending on the result, one learns something about that person, grows closer to the truth and widens one's mental horizon. By mistrusting a person, one may never find out if this mistrust was justified (p. 123). Gandhi might criticize Zittlau's interpretation of trust as a strategy, because Gandhi never used nonviolence as a strategy. He lived it because he believed it was right (Gandhi, 2003, p. 122). Rosenberg too, thinks it is important to trust in the good of every human. He states that people are easily vulnerable and hurt due to their own mistrust. The assumption that people may want to humiliate or rip others off can cause anger and makes it impossible to experience empathy (Rosenberg, 2009, p. 135). A lack of empathy advances the occurrence of violence. (For more about empathy see the relevant section on page 112).

Reactive and proactive nonviolence

Mahatma Gandhi differentiates between the reactive and proactive use of nonviolence. He considers both forms to be important. Reactive nonviolence appears as an answer to a certain event. It gained popularity through the works of Mahatma Gandhi and Martin Luther King, who both acted in response to the discrimination in their countries. Proactive nonviolence means "cultivating the sensibilities and compassion needed to respect others and their needs so that we can live in harmony" (Gandhi, 2003, p. 124). Another point of proactive nonviolence is what Mahatma Gandhi calls *trusteeship*. According to him, everyone is a trustee of the talents and resources given to him, individually as well as collectively. The trustee's responsibility is to exploit and use those talents for the welfare of all (p. 124-125). In the current survey 3, 85% of the people polled (rather) agreed that talents should be used for the welfare of everyone.

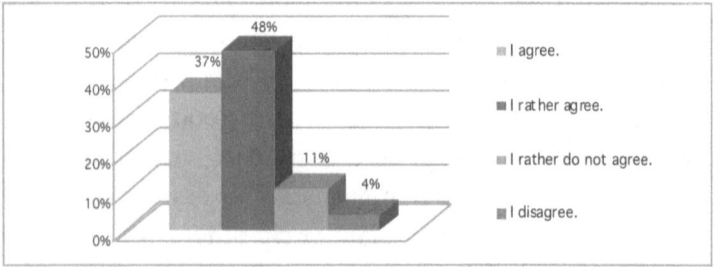

Fig. 8: *Agreement degree on whether talents should be used for the welfare of all. Survey 3, app. D.*

They argued that talents give their owners power and privileges which come with responsibility. People argued further that the development of talents was necessary for society's development. Some stated that the development of talents for the welfare of everyone also helped personal development. Some doubted whether it was possible to do something that led to welfare for everyone. Others pointed out that possessing the free will to do so was a condition. The people who (rather) not agreed stated that a talent could be a curse and that people who do not like their own talents should not have to develop them. One person was of the opinion that by using talents for the welfare of others limits one's free development (cf. App. D). An important aspect that probably was sometimes neglected is that everyone's welfare also includes one's own personal welfare. The consensus of the evaluation is that many people agreed with Gandhi on this point. The question that was not asked is whether these people who agreed do actually try to develop their talents for the welfare of everyone.

Nonviolence and the family

Genuine respect is a condition and an outcome of nonviolence and implicates the understanding of others as well as the acceptance and appreciation of their differences (Gandhi, 2003, p. 127). Such respect is very important for successful family life. Gandhi states that there can be no respect for society when there is no respect for the family, and a society is only as cohesive and loving as the families in it. He criticizes the materialistic and self-centered upbringing of children who often learn very early that success is only measured by material values. Further, Gandhi criticizes the trend of children being more of a by-product of sex than a couple's wish to raise a family together (p. 128-129). Due to the importance of family for the overall wellbeing of society, creating a family friendly working environment is thus a critical element and task of a nonviolent culture in an organization.

Nonviolence and truth

Gandhi (2007) states that nonviolence and truth are inseparably linked, just as violence and untruth are (p. 36). A lie is very common in business life, often for example, told to enhance the view of one's own products or devalue those of the competition. Some lies even seem essential to companies such as an untruth told about why an invoice had not yet been paid.

The author noted that 'little' lies told to outsiders are accepted within the company investigated, whereas amongst employees themselves, lying was not tolerated. On the contrary, only 7% of the people who answered the questionnaire were of the opinion that there was no possibility of getting along without telling lies at work (or school or studies). The opinion that work life is possible without lies does not necessarily mean that those people never lie at work. According to the results of a study by the sociologist Albert Vrij in Zittlau (2003), people lie on average twice a day (p. 55). In Survey 3, 70% of the people answered that they always tried to tell the truth. It could not be measured how hard they tried nor whether they actually lied twice a day, as Vrij revealed, or not. Besides, 40% were of the opinion that white lies are permissible[1] but here again white lies were not defined. Some use white lies already when they are in danger of getting into trouble with the boss, whilst others would use them to protect an endangered friend. The results from this survey seem to demonstrate that speaking truthfully is still seen as a value in German society.

Truth in business does not only mean not telling lies. According to Zittlau, the use of truth in business means, for example, that messages should be precise, unequivocal and complete. He states that innumerable office

---

1 cf. App. D.

hours are wasted because of confusing terminology and circuitous or overly eloquent assignments. Truth is not only a condition for nonviolence, it is actually useful in business life particularly, for example, in negotiations. Zittlau states that someone who really seeks truth can hardly be lied to. Mahatma Gandhi is the best example of that observation. Even his bitterest enemies admitted that they could never lie to Gandhi's face (p. 57-61).

The nonviolent culture

All these aspects of nonviolence seem to make a real nonviolent culture impossible. Nevertheless, Gandhi is of the opinion that love and nonviolence belong to man's nature and can thus be learnt by everyone even if not everyone will be able to practice it perfectly (Gandhi, Merton and Kurlansky, 2007, p. 35). There are several indicators that demonstrate that Gandhi is correct. David Loye, social psychologist and evolutionary modeler, analyzed Darwin's evolutionary theory. He discovered that the *survival of the fittest* appeared twice in the *Evolution of Man*, whilst, on the contrary, the term *love* appeared 95 times (Lindemann and Heim, 2010, p. 25). Handy (1999) gives examples which show that it is in man's nature to care for others. Parents make sacrifices for their children and people even fight or die for affairs from which they receive no direct payoff for themselves (p. 126). Lindemann and Heim (2010) refer to Joachim Bauer, neurobiologist and psychotherapist, who proved that biologically the human's brain responds to the success of relationships. When relationships are successfully created, the brain releases certain *pleasure chemicals* (p. 25).

A nonviolent culture is not a method which can be used for motivational means, nor is it a concept that can be used for instruction. It requires creativity to develop and develops creativity, as will be shown in later chapters. Furthermore, nonviolence has so many facets that one can hardly refer to all of them. Therefore, only a few aspects such as inspiration are mentioned.

Meeting people's needs

Lindemann and Heim (2010) write of some examples of how work environments can meet people's needs. In regard to *autonomy* as a need, they list some conditions which must exist in a workplace such as self-apportioning of work, achievement of one's own goals, and the allowance for individualized decision-making. Another example they name is structure and clarity. Conditions for these points are transparency, abidance to agreements, being included, reliability, peace, harmony and collegiality (p. 60). The conditions for these and other aspects of a nonviolent culture can be created through a structure which allows the conditions for meeting people's needs in the workplace.

No enemies

In a nonviolent culture there are no enemies. According to Gandhi, learning to build and cultivate good relationships, even with those who one would too easily call an enemy, is a basic condition of a nonviolent culture. Therefore it is important to understand how anger and conflicts occur. Conflicts ending with people seeing the other as an enemy are usually created when each party is only concerned about their own desires and demands and without respect for their opponent's needs. This topic will be taken up again in the section entitled *Conflict management* on page 104. Mahatma Gandhi (2003) states, "An eye for an eye only makes the whole world blind" (p. 122-123). Covey is of the opinion that competitors, for example, can be seen as friends who tell you where your weaknesses lie. They are a learning source, not an enemy. With the loss of an enemy, revenge also becomes unnecessary.

Forgiveness

The fact that no one can be perfectly nonviolent should not keep people from trying. Edmund Burke (Irish orator, philosopher, & politician) states that "no one could make a greater mistake than he who did nothing because he could do only a little."[1] In his opinion it is better to start action knowing it probably will not be much or be perfect than not even trying. Because nobody can be perfectly nonviolent, Gandhi (2003) sees forgiveness as essential for human life. Forgiveness liberates humans from the burden of hatred and revenge and it gives a culprit the chance to evaluate his actions (p. 21). Handy (1999) states that forgiveness is also important for the ability to learn. If people are afraid of punishment they will not risk even a little mistake and will remain beneath their potential (p. 127). Thus in the next chapter will be dealing with the subject of mistake-friendliness.

Having a mistake-friendly attitude

Another aspect of a nonviolent culture is the value-adding and the learning-promoting handling of mistakes. Martin Weingart (2004) defines mistakes as when a subject names an alternative as a *mistake*, when it is judged by him in relation to the correlative context to be so unfavorable that it seems to him to be unwanted (p.

---

1   Burke (year unknown).

292). This definition describes a *mistake* as a judgement which provides a favorable alternative to an unfavorable one on the basis of the subjective context.

According to Orth, mistakes are windows to life because when someone does something in a different way than everybody else or different from the way which standards define, (which is considered to be *wrong* or a *mistake*), one can learn a lot about or from this person. This *mistake* shows a different point of view concerning a certain action (p. 6). So, mistakes can help evolve creativity, advance learning and widen one's mental horizon. The author experienced this in her own company when once sending spare parts to a customer in Turkey. Although she accidentally did not fill in an A.TR (a document required by customs authorities) the shipment got to the customer without any problems, creating the realization that customs authorities were not as strict concerning low-value shipments. Thus, future low-value shipments were sent without an A.TR and effort was saved.[1]

At the company being investigated, most people at all hierarchical levels usually admitted their mistakes. Indeed, rather there seemed more likely to be a search for solutions even if they were not accomplished consequentially.

German society is very much marked by the thought that mistakes are something negative which need to be

1 cf. App. G.

avoided. Thomas von Kempen in Wingart (2004) describes this belief quite well in the quotation from Medieval times, *He, who does not avoid little mistakes, will shortly lapse into bigger ones* (p. 11). As an aside, perhaps von Kempen was not so much focused on mistakes as on the need to pay attention to small issues as well as the larger ones.

The technical development of Western culture has lead to the problem that mistakes can become deadly, for example when driving a car or handling nuclear technology. This could be one of many reasons why the attitude that mistakes are something negative is so acknowledged in society and especially in the educational system. But in society, as well as in the economy, this kind of thinking is beginning to be reconsidered, at least when it comes to less deadly mistakes. In Survey 3, 37% of the people interviewed were of the opinion that everyone should be encouraged not to make grave mistakes in life and 59% admitted to getting angry when they made a mistake. This seems to underpin the thesis that many people in German society see mistakes as something rather negative. However, despite the rather negative attitude towards mistakes, 59% were of the opinion that making mistakes is human and everyone is allowed to make them. 56% thought that it is only all right to make mistakes when you learn from them and do not repeat them.[1]

1 cf. App. D.

Violence vs. Nonviolence

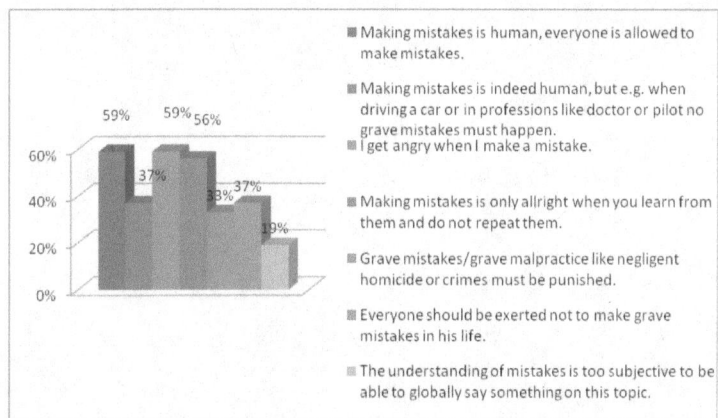

Fig. 9: Opinions on mistakes. Survey 3, app. D.

In the above-mentioned survey, 37% of the people were of the opinion that grave mistakes with deadly consequences should be avoided, e.g. when driving a car or flying a plane. This opinion invites the wider discussion of whether people with a lot of responsibility are not allowed to make mistakes in the same way as everyone else because their mistakes could cause irreparable damage. This topic will not be discussed more deeply in this book as it is not possible to predict how great the impact of such a mistake would actually be. Even the smallest action sometimes can have incalculable, negative consequences.

Leadership for a Nonviolent Culture

As framed in the section *The exertion of influence on organizational culture* on page 36, leadership is essential to take influence on an organization's culture. Therefore, this chapter will deal with the role of a leader and different types of leadership styles, as well as the possible tasks of a leader required to create a nonviolent culture. On page 32, the statement of Edward Simon was cited, "Business is the only institution that has a chance, [...] to fundamentally improve the injustice that exists in the world." This quotation continues, "... but first, we will have to move through the barriers that are keeping us from being truly vision-led and capable of learning." (Senge, 1990, p. 5). This statement frames the two important topics which leadership has to deal with in order to create a nonviolent culture namely, *vision lead* and *learning*.

Vision

First of all, such questions have to be posed as, 'Why does the company exist?' 'Why do people create social and productive systems called companies?' 'For what reason does my organization exist?' 'What does the company want to create?' These questions are particularly essential because they give meaning to what employees in the company do. Senge quotes Nietzsche who states that it is the *why* which is more important than the *how* because it makes people endure things. But it is the *why* which is usually harder to discover (Handy, 1990, p. 101).

"He who has a *why* to live can bear almost any *how*."

Friedrich Nietzsche

The creation and implementation of a strong vision is an important part of influencing the culture because, to a certain extent, the vision even defines the culture. The different definitions of culture have something in common. Culture has to do with the way people think and the way they are used to doing things. Some even include values under 'basic assumptions'.[1] Covey (2003) states that "culture, by definition, assumes shared vision and values" (p. 165).

---

1 See page 14.

Leadership for a Nonviolent Culture

Definitions of vision and mission

Gölzner (2006) points out that the understanding of vision and mission in German speaking countries and American understanding in general is not the same. In German speaking regions, a vision is a clear picture of the future, which defines basic goals. In America however, a vision statement is a more detailed description of the organizational situation in 3-5 years time. A mission statement in America according to Gölzner is an organization guideline (p. 85). Hitt et al (2008) define vision and mission, "Vision is a picture of what a firm or company wants to be and, in broad terms, what it ultimately wants to achieve." The mission's definition is more focused on the environment. "A mission specifies the business or businesses in which the firm intends to compete and the customers it intends to serve" (pp. 18-19). Drucker in Swaim (2009) defines vision and mission with these two questions: "What is our business?" (Mission) and "What should our business be?" (Vision). According to Drucker, a mission must always be linked to a company's customers, while a vision is focused on the organization itself and its strategic course (pp. 17-23).

Covey (2003) states that a mission statement is the representation of an organization's values and its shared vision (p. 165). According to Senge (1990), "a shared vision is the answer to the question, 'What do we want to create?'" (p. 206). This definition goes further than the previous ones because it is not limited to an ideal status of the organization.

These various definitions show clearly that there is no universal definition of vision and mission. The vision definitions all have something in common: Vision is a long-term view of an ideal future state of the organization or on a larger scale like society which leads to the strategic direction of an organization. Senge's broad definition of vision (answer to the question, 'What do we want to create') will be required for further discussion on vision because a nonviolent culture does not only focus on itself but includes the environment on which it has an effect. The understanding of mission presented in this paper is based upon the above mentioned definitions as:

> *Mission is the answer to the question: 'How do we want to achieve our vision?'*

Vision to inspire people

John Lennon's song *Imagine*, written in 1971 has fascinated, inspired and even united people all over the world for several decades. It has been on number one hit-lists in many countries, has won prizes and been recorded by dozens of artists. Its fascination can be due to its great vision of a social, peaceful world without religion, capitalism and patriotism.[1] The chorus of John Lennon's *Imagine* (1971) is undoubtedly familiar to most readers and is in essence very much based on the idea that if we want to have an ideal world in which everyone has a share then we have to start dreaming it. Dreams only come true if you have them in the first

---

1   Ruhlmann (year unknown).

place!

Senge (1990) states that there is hardly such a powerful force in human matters as a shared vision (p. 206). With respect to Senge's opinion, a strong shared vision can release enormous human potential and for a shared vision to succeed in business, both nonviolence and efficiency are essential ingredients.

Vision as a leading force

The efficiency of an organization is very much dependent on how much its members work in the same direction or, in other words, whether they share the same vision. This might be one reason for the success of many non-profit organizations. Most of them have a very strong vision and mission in which their members believe and which therefore motivates them at work (cf. Drucker, 2003, p. 41).

Covey (2003) criticizes the lack of shared vision and values in most companies. According to him, many companies have a mission statement but it is scarcely a part of their culture because employees are neither involved in creating it nor do they deeply understand it. Covey states that it is one of the 'chronic problems' in organizations. According to him, the loss of truly represented and deeply shared values and visions often leads to the other six of the seven 'chronic problems'[1] in organiza-

---

1 The seven chronic problems of an organization according to Covey are: 1. No shared vision and values, 2. No strategic path, 3. Poor alignment, 4. Wrong style, 5. Poor

tions (pp. 165-172). Drucker too, is of the opinion that it is a basic task of a leader to make sure that everyone knows, understands and lives the mission.[1]

According to Collins (2009), a mission statement builds a bridge between the basic tensions of modern organizations as interplay between continuance and change. An organization with a strong mission knows what is not to be changed—the values and purposes defined in the mission statement – and builds the needed change around it. This requires also knowing what must not be done when it does not fit into the mission statement. So, in Collin's opinion, a mission statement is an important guideline in a fast changing world (pp. 47-49).

Vision in the Investigated Company

Vision and mission were introduced some years ago when a consultant advised to do so. During that time, having a vision was 'in' and a kind of obligation for a company in order that it might better distinguish itself from the competition. Yet the investigator, who had been an employee for almost three years, had never heard of the vision and it was not until she asked that she received any information about it. She was told that the vision and mission had fallen into oblivion. Instead of a vision and mission, a company philosophy had come to the fore. The philosophy was stated on the company's homepage as follows:

---

skills, 6. Low trust, 7. No integrity.
1   cf. Drucker (1999) p. 14-16.

Through the quality of our durable products and services we attain customer satisfaction.

The sky is the limit and we set ourselves no boundaries and maintain a worldwide sales network being both local and global at the same time.

We place great emphasis on our national culture which is known for its modesty, honesty and diligence.

Our motivated employees are dedicated and highly qualified employees and our paramount assets.

We wish to attain continuous sustainable growth whilst providing value to customers and employees alike.

This philosophy is supposed to tell people how to do things in a similar way as a mission would.

There are several points in the philosophy which can be subjected to criticism. Firstly, there are many superficial words contained in it and they are open to a variety of interpretations. There are a number of undefined concepts such as quality, durable products, low prices, good service, environmentally friendly production, value (which poses the question of what is meant by value) and the saying, *the sky is the limit* (without defining what the limit is or what action can be expected from it). In a discussion with the human resource manager[1] it became clear, that *the sky is the limit*, for example, meant that the company is open for new ideas, it has multifarious products, develops new products and custom builds. Quality and value were once defined in a company presentation but these definitions were not available to everyone who

1 cf. App. G.

read the philosophy.

Covey (2003) writes on values that they are, contrary to principles, internal and therefore subjective (p. 19). The term *value* does not explain itself and therefore is not adequate for a philosophy addressed to external people.

Today, many companies use the following phrase which is included in the above, such as, 'Our employees are our most important asset'. This statement might be meant as an appreciation of the employees but as long as they are looked upon as *assets*, they are mainly seen as cost factors. This view prevents true love which, according to Gandhi, is a condition for nonviolence and is also therefore essential for a nonviolent culture.[1] A nonviolent leader leads his people with love which, according to Marcic (1997), is also a condition for efficient leadership. Marcic criticizes that bosses and consultants go into organizations with their formulas and strategies but without love. She points out that these means can hardly work properly without love and they can even inflict harm (pp. 18-19). She states that many leaders in organizations do not manage to get their people to work efficiently because they have not figured out "some of these basic principles of operating with other humans"(p. 18).

A point which is not mentioned in the above-mentioned philosophy (unless local society comes under the term *customer*) is that the organization takes on some responsibility for the local society. Employment preference

---

1 cf. page 55.

is given to people who live in the area and machine parts are mostly bought from local producers. Additionally the local community benefits from taxation, depending on the company's success and, for example, from its donations to the local school.

Although the philosophy is quite well known at the company (66% know its content and 29% have once heard about it)[1], one of the department managers criticized the lack of vision and the managerial problems this had caused several times. He mentioned that proactive action and long-term development are affected adversely by the lack of vision.[2]

The vision that existed (or had existed) cannot really be called a vision according to the previous definitions on page 71ff. The exposed vision and mission were as follows:

> *As a provider of high quality systems for handling products we are market leader in many areas. We have a balanced value system where, whilst not perfect, we see that unavoidable mistakes are the price of progress*

In the company's vision there is no picture of the future, nothing the company wants to achieve. It is a description of what it is and how things are done in the company. The word *vision* contains seeing or viewing something. Therefore every vision should be expressible in a picture (a metaphor).

1 cf. App. B.
2 cf. App. C.

Creation and implementation of strong vision

According to Senge (1990), a strong vision pushes the person who has the vision forward whilst the actual situation is pulling him backwards (p. 151). The vision should not be too easily attainable because then the *creative tension* (which pulls people in a certain direction) gets lost. On the other hand, it should not be unattainable or unrealistic because if people do not believe in it, it will also lose its attraction.

Actual situation — Shared Vision

Fig. 10: Creative tension with shared vision. (Based on Senge (1990) p. 151.)

According to Senge, there are only a few people in contemporary organizations who really put energy into a vision based on their convictions, what he calls *enrollment*. An *enrolled* person is part of something because he wants to be such, whilst most organizational members are only compliant to the vision, only carrying it to a certain extent because it is expected of them. Real commitment is quite rare in organizations. People who really commit to the vision have the aim to reach for it, whatever structures are needed (pp. 218-219).

According to Covey (2003), a vision should include these four basic needs (p. 166):

1. Economic or money need
2. Social or relationship need

3. Psychological or growth need
4. Spiritual or contribution need

Because these four points are basic human needs, they will quite probably appeal to people but none of them could be found in the vision of the company being investigated.

According to Drosdek (2007), the best way to convince people of something is to let them participate in the decision-making process (p. 54). To make sure the vision is carried and lived by everyone due to their own conviction, it is necessary to involve all organizational members in its creation.

According to internal information, there were times when vision played an important role and people thought about it many times. After placing so much emphasis on the vision, people got tired of that 'vision stuff'. By getting tired of it, people were never really enrolled and inspired by the vision. There is practically no vision and a huge lack in the culture of the company. It weakens the company or as Covey puts it, the company has got a *chronic problem*.[1]

---

1 cf. page 73ff.

Motivational models

Motivating people is an important leadership task and necessary to create a nonviolent culture. Only motivated people are willing to learn and to take over responsibility. Therefore this whole chapter will deal with motivation of people in organizations.

Maslow's hierarchy of needs

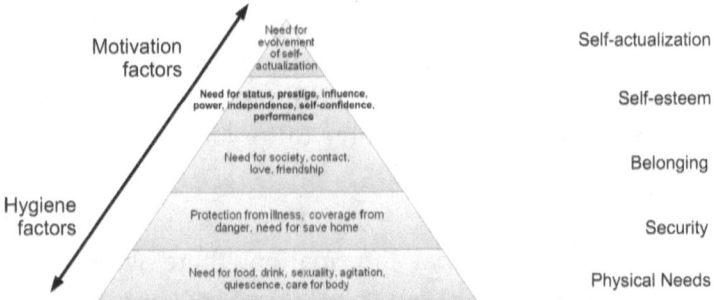

Fig. 11: *Maslow's pyramid of needs with Herzberg's motivation-hygiene theory. (Based on Maslow, quoted in Lorenz and Rohrschneider (2007) p. 84.)*

According to Maslow's hierarchy of needs (developed 1954), a need is only a motivator as long as it is unsatisfied. It is also assumed that the satisfaction of lower needs is the condition for the pursuit of higher needs. The lower needs are basics for survival, therefore it makes sense that they are the ones which human beings usually try to satisfy first (Lorenz and Rohrschneider, 2007, p. 85). To know what can be motivating for an organization member, the leader first must know at which level that person stands yet to be able to know at which level an employee is, a leader has to know his people personally. Due to the small sections, department managers at the firm in question usually knew their colleagues personally. On the other hand, the personal contact between head management and employees had been somewhat restricted during recent years.

One criticism of this interpretation of Maslow is that it is not necessarily true that basic needs have to be met before the higher needs can be satisfied. In fact, the evidence of people like Gandhi seem to demonstrate in example that people with a vision and strong sense of self-actualization (or higher needs not included in Maslow's model) will often be willing to forsake the fulfillment of basic needs for this higher goal.

Herzberg's motivation-theory

Herzberg developed another motivation-theory known as the 'Two Factor Theory' which differentiates between *hygiene factors* and *motivators*. Hygiene factors must be met to avoid dissatisfaction while the motivators lead to satisfaction and therefore have a motivating effect.

Hygiene factors	Motivation factors / Motivators
- Company policy - Supervision - Relationship with boss - Work conditions - Salary - Relationship with colleagues	- Achievement - Recognition - Work itself - Responsibility - Advancement - Growth

Table 3: Hygiene factors and motivation factors according to Herzberg's two factor theory. (Based on Herzberg, quoted in Lorenz / Rohrschneider (2007) p. 86.)

Usually hygiene factors and motivators are ordered as in the table above but according to circumstances, different factors can appear as hygiene factors or motivators. A possible risk of this model could be the tendency to treat everyone in a similar way even though hygiene factors and motivators differ from person to person because of everyone's differing needs (cf. ibid p. 86).

Money as a means of motivation

Money has got a high attractiveness due to its omnipotence which means that it can be used for almost every kind of exchange and money can be transformed into products or services (Theobald, 2009, p. 164). Money is never a need. It is a strategy or medium with which to fulfill needs such as the need for food, shelter and security, which can be satisfied with the help of money (Rosenberg, 2009, p. 157). Handy (1999) states that the desire for money can function as a substitute for something else (p. 110) like an unsatisfied need. As the social-scientists Campbell, Converse and Willard revealed in their study 'Quality of American life', one's financial situation only marginally contributes to a person's contentment. A sensation was caused by the study carried out by The London School of Economics and Political Science in 1998. According to the happiness-rating in that study, people in Bangladesh, Azerbaijan, Nigeria, India and the Philippines were the happiest. The industrial nations were a lot less happy. While people in Great Britain were in position 32, Germans reached position 42 in global comparison. The USA only reached position 46, although they quote the quest for happiness in their independence declaration from 1776 (cf. Theobald (2009) p. 166).

Economists suppose that the rate of money and happiness follows the rule of diminishing marginal utility. This means that an income of 100,000 EUR a year makes a higher contribution to happiness than one of 10,000 EUR but not ten times as much. In the survey entitled 'The Psychology of Happiness' by the English social psychologist Michael Argyl, 67% of multi-millionaires considered themselves to be happy, whilst 62% of average income earners also classified themselves as being happy. Handy (1990) explains this phenomenon as, "Maybe money is a necessary but not sufficient condition of happiness."(p. 6).

Fortune scientist Easterlin created a survey on how much extra money people needed to make themselves happy. The answer was: Around 20% (Theobald, 2009, p. 165).

These studies show quite clearly that money as a motivating factor only works to a certain extent. Once the needs of the first and maybe second levels of Maslow's Pyramid of Purposes are satisfied, needs on a higher level occur which cannot be satisfied by an income increase. Where money is the only motivational factor that keeps an employee in the company, it is probable that there is no strong loyalty from the employee towards the company. Therefore, if the employee was to receive a better financial offer from another company he is likely to leave.

Exactly this happened at the company in question. One of the employees asked for a higher salary several times but the answer she received was only that it would be considered. Half a year later she left because another company offered her more money.[1]

Money can even have a negative effect on motivation. What counts very much is the comparison with others. Theobald (2009) refers to the example of driving an expensive car. As soon as the neighbor has the same one, is looses its personal value. This phenomenon occurs in a similar way with income. An example is the case of an employee who received around 3,000 EUR per month

---

1 cf. App. G.

and was content with his income. However, when he realized that his colleague was receiving more money for, in the employee's opinion, less work, the contentment towards his income decreased dramatically.[1] Anyone who feels that he is treated in an unfair way easily becomes dissatisfied (p. 165). This aspect also became apparent in the firm which was the subject of our research. It was desired that people should be constantly involved in an improvement process, especially in the improvement of technical issues on machines. For any good ideas considered worth playing out, people received a certain amount of extra money. However, people very often felt unfairly treated because of disputes about which ideas were actually considered worth putting into practice. Their motivation dropped through dissatisfaction when their idea was not rewarded as hoped. Therefore this system was eventually abolished.

Motivation in the company

People in the company mainly seemed to want to be motivated monetarily. There was little request for the means of motivation through such methods as job enrichment, job enlargement, more freedom or more responsibility at work. Target agreements, bonuses and higher salary were the most requested means. This occurrence brings up the question as to why this is the case when, according to several management thinkers, money is no means for truly motivating people. One reason might be that people are not really aware of their actual needs or how to fulfill them. Another consideration

1   cf. App. G.

could be that there is no offer that can truly fulfill the employee's intrinsic needs at work. Acting as a substitute, the extra money will help them to meet their needs in everyday life instead. At the company in question there were many people over 50 years of age, especially in the manufacturing department. This aspect suggests the explanation that many elderly people are very security conscious and therefore prefer more money instead of say, job enrichment, as this will enhance their pension rights. This also may reveal that when considering employee motivation, managers give to little attention to with private agenda concerns. It could well be that because an employee cannot gain real intrinsic motivation in the workplace, that he seeks this satisfaction in private life and this may seem to require money for its fulfillment.

Another possible explanation for this occurrence is offered by the effort and gain model.

Effort and gain model

An assumption of the effort-gain model is that people only perform well long-term, if they are motivated intrinsically (motivators of Herzberg's model). The model also assumes that people feel that work is effort, for example home-to-office time, arguments with colleagues, struggle and so on. On the other side of the coin is the gain people get from work. The term gain does not mean money. It means topics like fun, learning, appreciation, status, influence, being among people and many other things (cf. Lorenz and Rohrschneider, 2007, pp. 89-91).

Leadership for a Nonviolent Culture

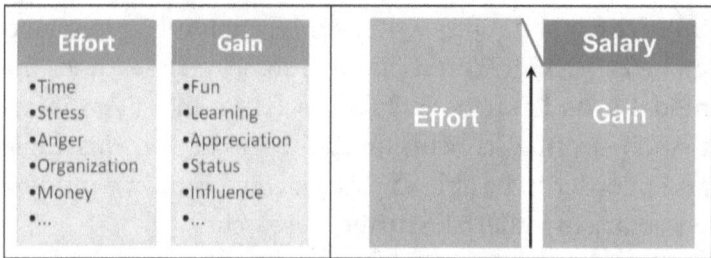

Fig. 12: Effort and Gain in an ideal state (left) and in a usual state (right). (Based on Lorenz and Rohrschneider (2007) p. 89.)

The left picture of the effort and gain model in the above diagram shows the ideal state where effort and gain are balanced. In the right of the diagram, effort outweighs gain. This gap is filled through salary. The diagonal line is the set point for satisfaction. With increasing imbalance between effort and gain, dissatisfaction in the company will grow.

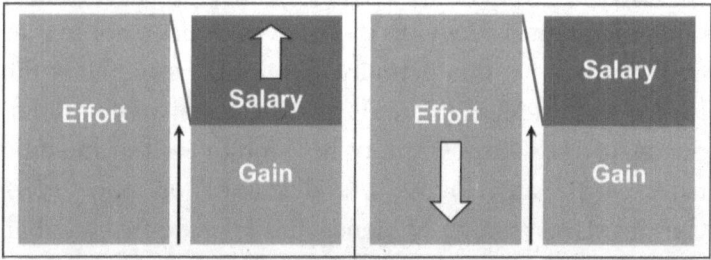

Fig. 13: Effort and gain model in a status of employee's dissatisfaction. (Based on Lorenz and Rohrschneider (2007) p. 90.)

The above diagram shows what happens when the imbalance between effort and gain is too high. First, an employee wants to get a higher salary as an alternative to real gain. In the next step he will lower his effort to adjust the unbalance (Lorenz & Rohrschneider, 2007, p. 90). Many of the company's employees often refused to accept extra effort without extra gain. This fact seems to lend support the Effort and Gain Model. It might be useful to think about just why people want to be motivated monetarily. One could hazard some guesses and the model does lend some clues. Based on the given information no final conclusion can be made on this topic and in order to be able to make a conclusion it would be necessary to undertake further research.

Motivation in a nonviolent culture

Everyone carries his own values into a company when they then come into contact with the culture of the organization. The more these values match with the organizational culture, the higher is the satisfaction and success of employees and the company (cf. Kreuzhof / Lambert, 2009, p. 8). Motivation in a nonviolent culture comes from leaders who want to help their organizations members to develop themselves. It does not matter that much how this actually happens. Essential is the leader's attitude. He cannot use the usual motivational means to get the most out of his employees but must be truly caring and loving. As discussed on page 55ff., Gandhi states that nonviolence and love are inseparable. According to Marcic (1997), people's behavior is the manifestation of their inner lives. Believing in Spiritual Laws (as Marcic calls this occurrence) or not, people will realize such love driven behavior and respond to it through their actions (pp. 8-9).

Nonviolent use of power

Power is very much afflicted with negative associations. A reason might be that in Western society people in very powerful positions often refuse to take over responsibility. Drucker (2003) clearly states that authority always demands responsibility. Power and responsibility are two sides of the same coin and therefore are not categorized separately. The other commonality is that whoever takes over responsibility always demands authority (p. 61). Lindemann and Heim (2010) mention Riane Eisler's book *The Chalice and the Blade*, in which she shows that almost all material and social technologies on which the western civilization is based were developed around ten thousand years ago. This time was embossed by an understanding of power as a means to serve the welfare of everyone (p. 23). Because a leader has a lot of power bestowed upon him by his job, it is essential to think deeply about the use of power.

Covey (2003) points out the coherence of effectiveness, power, violence and the condition of one's mind. He states that the requirement of being highly effective is that a person's conscience is able to control all he imagines, envisions and engineers.

The exercise of creativity without conscience inevitably leads to the unconscionable. Therefore, creative power must come with social responsibility and conscience (p. 43).

Rosenberg (2009) differentiates between two different ways of using power, the *protective* and *castigatory* use of power. The *protective* use of power is lead by the goal to prevent injustice and hurt by another. By using power protectively, one's attention is focused on the life, rights and welfare of another person without judging that person or his behavior. The *Castigatory* use of power utilizes power to make others suffer for what they have done wrong in the acting person's opinion. This kind of power-use tries to push a person in a certain direction through punishment, for example. But punishment has its price. When the motivation of an action is to escape punishment, the affected person's attention is distracted from the original work (pp, 181-183). In a nonviolent culture, punishment is out-of-place. Dawtry writes about the sources of crime and violence in modern times and he concludes that punishment does not meet the cause of erratic behavior. Dawtry (1962) is of the opinion that a lot of violent action is the result of pressure from modern society on individuals and instead of being punishing, people should be trained. Just like disabled people who do not really 'fit in', society should try to integrate the morally and socially inadequate who have committed crime and acted violently. To point out such a person's abnormality will make him realize his being different and even give him a feeling of justification of his action. Instead, this individual must be accepted the way he is and be helped to understand his feelings, actions and the problems he has (pp. 29-30). Questioning people on their opinion as to whether grave malpractice such as negligent homicide or crimes should be punished, one third of those questioned agreed.[1] This opinion is based on western world black and white thinking of good people and those people who are bad whereby the latter are deserving of punishment. This 'judge-mental' model ad-

1 cf. App. D.

vances violence as discussed previously in the chapter *Causes of violence*, p. 42ff.

The nonviolent use of money

Haller (1990) points out that money gives power to its owner. By deciding what a person's money will be invested in, the owner can give life to destructive happenings, objects or inventions. On the contrary it can be used to create welfare for many. For example, an idea can only become reality if the resources are available which are needed to materialize it, such as the people who work on it, the materials used to produce it and so on. So financial assets are the fuel to make human ideas become reality (pp. 84-85). A related example is the wars which are fought over resources and which are only profitable as long as there are customers to buy those resources.

Haller states that the making anonymous of monetary flow through the banks makes it hard for investors to exert influence over what their money is used for (p.86). Nevertheless, the power of the customer should not be underestimated and if enough customers wish to know what happens with their money, change could be brought about. Although 56% of the questioned people in survey 3 answered that it mattered to them what their money was used for, only 19% of them believed that they knew the answer. 78% of them stated that they would choose a different bank or bank deposit if they knew that their money was invested in something of which they disapproved. In the process of asking these questions, many people admitted that they had never thought about these topics.[1] In the German cultural world, talking about money is not very common, neither in private life nor in business (cf. Henke, 2009). In a nonviolent culture getting people to think about their exposure to money might be an important issue. The handling of the organization's assets might be discussed and reflected in the mission or in the organization's principles as discussed in the section *Principle-centered leadership* on page 95ff. This could have two positive effects namely, responsible handling of money in the organization and also perhaps getting people thinking about their handling of money in their private lives.

An example of a bank which considers nonviolence in its investments is the Steyler Bank. In its ethical concept, the Steyler Bank states that all investment forms are examined. They are tested on environmental issues, protection of human dignity and what they do for society. The concept also includes the statement that they are of the opinion, that every single company has responsibility and carries the human and moral consequences for its economic decisions. [...] Companies, who threaten peace, justice and the creation do not get money from the Steyler Bank. This is a consequential example of the responsible and nonviolent use of money.[2]

---

1 cf. App. D.
2 cf. https://www.steyler-bank.de

Servant leadership

According to Greenleaf (1977), a really great leader's nature is to be a servant, which is the aspect that represents his greatness (p. 21). There have been good examples that sustain or even prove Greenleaf's statement on leader as a servant. The most famous examples are Jesus of Nazareth, Mahatma Gandhi or Martin Luther King.

Because humans are the only creatures that have the power and the freedom to make choices, they have, according to Greenleaf, "natural authority over all creation. (p. 5)" Due to their authority and power, all people have responsibility for their environment and fellow creatures. They should thus use their power in a principled way. If a whole culture would live according to moral authority, there would be no need for laws. A principle-centered leader will automatically develop moral authority (p. 5).

Greenleaf is of the opinion that moral principles emerge from experience rather than developing out of theory and that the chance of their development is higher in an environment when the three circumstances shown in the following table are present:

Principles friendly environment	Development of principle friendly environment at company
Concern for justice rather than for order	Rather not present due to actual situation (crisis). Senses of justice varies, justice should be defined first.
Concern for performance rather than the form	The form is not unchangeable. There is space for individual performance improvement. Nevertheless often the form stays the same at the performance's cost because people are too easy-going or because they feel threatened by change.
Concern for the appropriateness rather than the result.	There is always the attempt to act appropriately but its priority is not higher than that of the result.

Table 4: Principles friendly environment according to Greenleaf and its development at the company under investigation. (Based on Greenleaf (2003) p. 33.)

Greenleaf talks of servant as leader instead of the other way round. The servant leader realizes the world's problems and accepts them as a personal task to achieve his own integrity. A servant stands in contrast to a "popular" leader, who will very probably prefer an easy solution and do what is expected of him at that moment. The servant quality often develops when a person is young. It is shaped rather by example than by precept (pp. 37-40. This underlines the importance of acting as an ideal, which is a central point in principle-centered leadership. Questioning leaders in our survey as to whether they understood their leadership style in the sense of serving, two out of three leaders agreed. They stated that serving is an important requirement in the company and in life. It serves the company's realization of goals, strategies and the vision. The person who negated the question argued that a leading activity needs to leave enough space for one's own creativity.[1] So, this person was of the opinion that serving narrows one's creativity.

Principle-centered leadership

In his book on Principle-Centered Leadership, Covey (2003) compares leadership with fishing. He states that a manager's job is to empower his employees., Covey expresses the meaning of empowerment using an old axiom: "Give a man a fish and you will feed him for a day. Teach him how to fish and you feed him for a lifetime. (p. 256)"

In the mental image of fishing, the stream illustrates the environment of an organization in which an employee 'fishes'. But the stream does not flow steadily. The environment changes constantly and more and more rapidly but people need something stable in their lives. Very often this stability is formed by the habits and lifestyle which have lead to success in the past. However, as the stream changes its direction and the response stays the same, the fish will not bite any more (pp. 313-319).

---

1 cf. App. C.

Gillett (1963) shows the danger of conservatism not only for organizations but for whole societies. As described on page 25ff., Gillett mentioned Arnold Toynbee's *A Study of History* in which Toynbee demonstrates how history has shown that wars have been the most common means to solve conflicts. Today, to attempt to resolve a conflict with the power of modern weapons such as with nuclear weapons could destroy the whole world. He compares this issue with the oft repeated story of David and Goliath which shows how strength leads to over-confidence and makes people unable to react to new circumstances (p. 8) or as Covey (2003) puts it, "nothing fails like success" (p. 8). Handy (1990) points out that people learn from mistakes, not from success. Having success after success, people get dull and their learning process gets handicapped (p. 55). Covey sees principle-centered leadership as an answer to changing environments (and many other 'problems').

Covey points out that principles are not a human invention but are natural laws such as is gravity in the physical dimension. Natural principles are similar to a compass, always showing the direction no matter how the environment changes. Covey states that natural laws and natural principles are objective and cannot be violated without consequences. By violating natural principles, people face the danger of disintegration and destruction. By living natural principles such as fairness, equality, integrity, honesty and trust, people move towards survival and stability, because principles are, according to Covey, the key to rich internal power (pp. 17-22). This internal power is "the foundation of culture. It aligns shared values, structures, and systems (p. 20)." Covey names security, guidance, wisdom and power as four fundamental and interacting dimensions of a life supporting system:

Security represents people's sense of worth, self-esteem, identity, emotional anchorage and personal strength.

Guidance is a direction people get in their lives. It comes not only from standards and principles but also from spiritual conscience and inspiring sources.

Wisdom is wholeness, a sense of balance, an understanding of how the principles and dimensions of life interact. Concretely this means getting and increasing a sense of the ideal (things as they should be) and the sensitive experience of reality (things as they are). Wisdom also contains the distinction of pure joy and temporary pleasure.

Power is the ability to act, to make decisions, to overcome deeply anchored habits. Powerful people have vision and discipline and have lives that are the outcome of their decisions rather than external conditions.

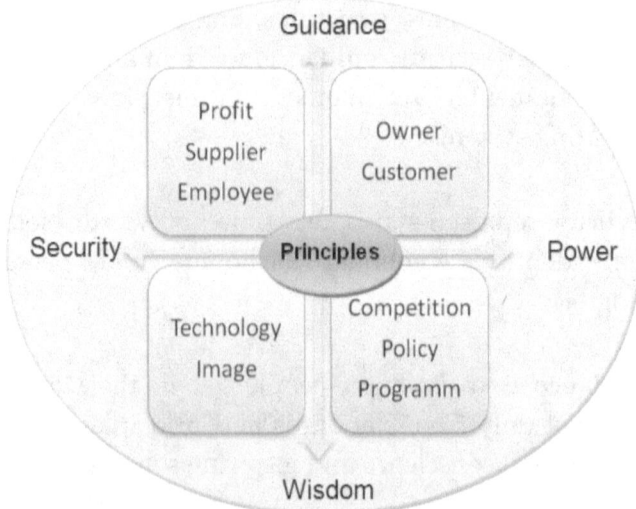

Fig. 14: Alternative center of a principle centered organization. (Based on Covey (2003) p. 24.)

Covey goes on to point out that focusing on alternate centers such as profit, customer, competition, image and so on is insufficient compared with principles as a center. For example: If image or cash flow are the reasons for an organization's security, leaders tend to feel threatened by the success and recognition of others and need the failure of competitors for their own satisfaction. On the other hand, if the weakness of others is the base for an organization's security, this weakness gets empowered to control that organization. Having principles in the center, it becomes clear that the only way to treat people, even the competition, is the same as you would want them to treat you. Competition can then be seen as a teacher pointing to an organization's weaknesses (pp. 23-25).

Principles and the nonviolent culture

Principles are supposed to be guidelines for life, to help people measure their own personal behavior. Kreuzhof and Lambert (2009) state that they are the starting point for a process of enhancement of leadership and the organizational culture (p. 6). Covey (2003) clearly points out that common attitude "Business is business", where ethics and principles are at most worth a backseat or are only for private life, is not valid (p. 15). Zittlau (2003) states that Gandhi underpinned the inseparability of work and private life. Gandhi was of the opinion that someone who violates his principles in business life cannot live them in private life either and the other way round (pp. 53-54). By abusing principles for judgment, they do not fulfill their original purpose, because judgment is a kind of violence. By categorizing things, happenings, people and so on in good and bad, one creates barriers between oneself and the others which contradicts a nonviolent philosophy (Gandhi, 2003, p. 23). Principles are necessary in order to create a nonviolent culture because this is a process which has to start from the inside out and cannot be forced from outside. It is, for example, not enough to train people in communication skills like listening and explaining. This effort of creating a nonviolent culture (Covey writes about a *cooperative* culture) in an organization will fail, in Covey's (2003) opinion. Unless these initiatives are based on common created principles instead of politics, people will resist these efforts in the long term (p. 118). Gandhi (2003) is of the same opinion and states that laws can only be effective if they enjoy the wide affirmation of the population. He states that laws are to a certain extent necessary but not sufficient as long as they carry no moral obligations alongside them. The reaction to laws without a moral backing in society is either tolerance by those who do not want struggle or counter-aggression. For any law to be effective, it needs moral appeal. The mentality of abiding by a law because people are convinced of its necessity is completely different from adherence due to the fear of penalty. This aspect is important for a nonviolent culture because it will not create decline and aggression (p. 126).

According to Covey (2003), the foundation of a principle-centered leadership and culture in an organization lies with people and their relationships (p. 118). Concerning relationships, Arun Gandhi states that building good relationships with others, even with those one does not like so much, is essential for a nonviolent culture (Gandhi, 2003, p. 123). So, principle-centered leadership is an important step for creating a nonviolent culture. An example for an organization with strong principles is the Mondcivitan Republic. More on this organization and its principles is posed in appendix F.

Characteristics of principle-centered leaders

Covey (2003) defines the following eight characteristics of people who were principle-centered leaders: They are continually learning, service oriented, radiate positive energy, believe in other people, lead balanced lives, see life as an adventure, they are synergistic and they exercise for self-renewal. He states that these characteristics show personal progress and signal effective leaders (pp. 33-39).

Being living examples of principles vested with these eight characteristics, a leader becomes a living ideal for his people. Covey states on principle-centered leadership: "The challenge is to be a light, not a judge; to be a model, not a critic p. 25)."

There are many reasons for the importance of being an ideal. According to Covey, it is the basis for influencing others in a powerful and ethical way. He designed the illustrated *Pyramid of Influence* with three basic categories (p. 119):

1. Modeling: To be an example that people can *see*.
2. Relating: To build caring relationships which people can *feel*.
3. Overt Attempt to Influence: To advise by instruction which people can *hear*.

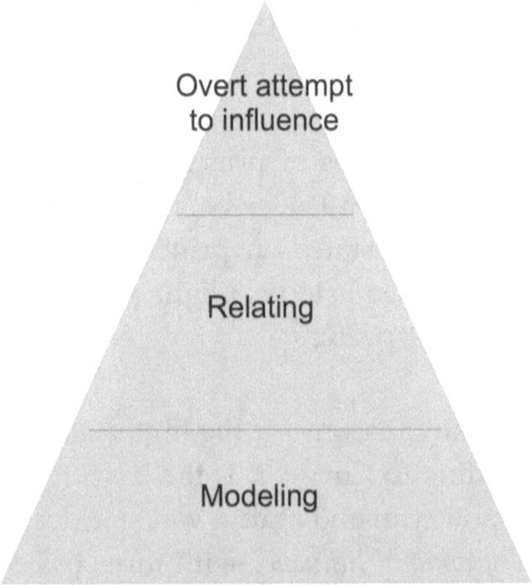

```
        Overt attempt
        to influence

            Relating

            Modeling
```

Fig. 15: Pyramid of influence. (Based on Covey (2003) p. 119.)

Another aspect of the importance of being a model is identified by Jay Cross, founder of the Internet-Time-Group. According to him, formal learning is improper for transforming knowledge into adequate action as it contributes less than 1% to change of behavior. People learn better by experience (cf. Bruhn and Hölzle, 2009, p. 28-29), and by the experience of the behavior of others. Another item is that acting as an ideal is a picture people are confronted with day by day. It is a picture they have in mind which can inspire them due to the energy of visualization (cf. Jumpertz, 2010, p. 56). As soon as it is expected of people that they should act in a certain way, the leader has to exemplify it. Otherwise, the reasons why they should act that way when the leader does not will be scarcely understood by employees. One of the authors remembers an experience whilst having the privilege of working with Wilhelm Haller, a great example of a servant as leader. A large package had been delivered to the company and left in the downstairs entrance hall. It needed to be taken up to the first floor yet nobody had felt responsible. So after waiting a day, Willi, (who was the CEO and extremely busy yet always found time for every individual) without saying a word, carried it up himself. Most of us felt ashamed as we could have done the same thing and a lesson was learnt by many on that occasion, that everybody should feel responsible for what needs doing.

"Being an ideal is not the most important way of influencing others. It is the only one." *Albert Schweitzer*[1]

Not only can leaders be an ideal. Every single member of an organization is to some extent an ideal for his colleagues. An ideal can be a negative influence as well as a positive one.

All managers who filled in the questionnaire of Survey 2 answered that they wanted to be an ideal in their private sphere as well as in their business life. Acting as an ideal seemed to be an important part of this company's culture but it had not been defined what these leaders considered as necessary action in order to become an ideal for others.

---

1   Our translation of the German: *Ein Beispiel zu geben ist nicht die wichtigste Art, wie man andere beeinflusst. Es ist die einzige*. Quoted in: Lindemann and Heim (2010) p. 42.

Creating a Non Violent Culture in the Workplace

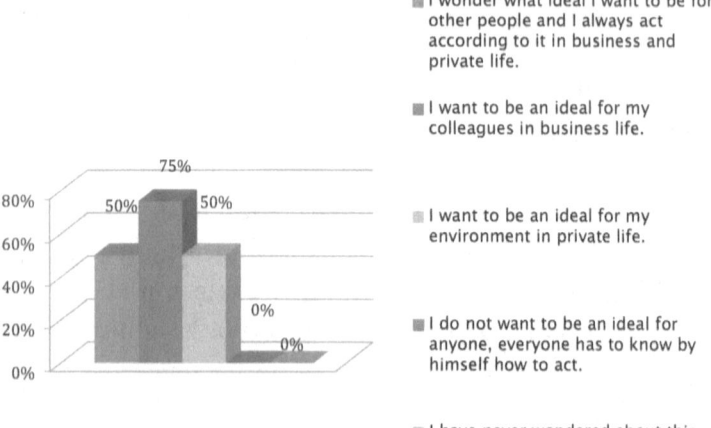

Fig. 16: Evaluation of the question "How do you see your function as an ideal?" cf. Survey 2, app. C.

Conflict management

Conflict costs

Conflicts are natural happenings when people converge (cf. Lindemann and Heim, 2010, p. 21). Nonviolence does not mean that conflicts must be avoided at any cost, the opposite is the case. Used in an efficient way, conflicts widen the horizon of the conflict parties allowing real exchange to happen. On the contrary, what causes huge damage are conflicts that are exposed too late or not at all. A survey on conflict costs by KPMG AG showed that in companies in Germany and Switzerland, conflict handling consumes 10–15% of the work time. For leaders, the time they spend directly or indirectly on conflict handling is 30-50% of their work time. Fluctuation, financial settlements and health costs caused by conflicts in companies cost several billion Euros a year. Every second company has costs around $75,000 for delayed projects due to conflicts.[1] According to the statements in Survey 1, most people at the company exposed existing conflicts quickly. In the same company survey, 29% of staff stated that they were confronted with conflicts almost weekly and 43% almost monthly. 28% stated that they were rarely confronted with conflicts. Most conflicts (73%) concerned interfaces between two areas of operation. Only 2% named personal reasons for a conflict. This is a very good basis for a nonviolent culture because, as explained in the chapter entitled *No enemies* on page 63ff., good relationships are essential for nonviolence. Yet this result may be seen critically because quite often a personal conflict is carried out on the factual level. In any case, most people (91%) stated that conflicts are always or usually being solved to the contentment of everyone without involving a third party.[2]

Conflict escalation

On the physical level, conflict escalation can be explained as follows: As soon as the opponent is seen as a threat, a human's brain switches to survival mode and rational thinking is blocked. The opponent is often seen as a threat, when needs are not satisfied and people are afraid not to be able to act freely and more. It does not matter whether this fear is justified or evolved out of other reasons like a misunderstanding. As soon as the brain is on 'survival mode' and the limbic system takes

1 Survey on conflict costs by KPMG Ag (2009).
2 cf. App. B.

control, one easily shows reactions like shouting, impeding, contact avoidance and so on.

To stay under better control and to be able to solve a conflict in an efficient way, one has to know about the reasons for one's own reactions as well as thoughts. Judgments and projections happen very quickly and very often unconsciously (cf. Lindemann and Heim, 2010, p. 30). Therefore it is important to train oneself to stay under control of one's own mind and not to succumb to over-reactions. In survey 3, 33% of the questioned people stated that sometimes they cannot control their anger.[1] Putliba Gandhi, Mahatma Gandhi's mother, is reported to have said "a mind that is out of control, is a devil's workshop" (Gandhi, 2003, p. 29). According to Gandhi, conflicts occur when there is no respect for the other person and everyone is only concerned about his own wishes and desires. The energy of anger often is used in a destructive way, advancing aggression and therefore violence (p. 123). This opinion is supported by Rosenberg (2009), who describes that if people receive a message as blame or judgment, they get angry and aggressive. To use a dispute in a constructive way, empathy for self and for the other person is necessary (pp. 115-117). The model of nonviolent communication, developed by Marshall Rosenberg, can help one stay calm in conflict situations and to get in touch with one's own needs as well as with the needs of the opponent. Because it emphasizes clear expression, it can help to clarify and even prevent misunderstandings which are a source of

---

1   cf. App. D.

many conflicts.

Nonviolent communication based on Marshall Rosenberg

Language is an important module of a nonviolent leadership-style and a nonviolent organizational culture. It influences human thinking which directs all of a person's actions. The goal of nonviolent communication is to build relationships based on openness and compassion by getting people in touch with their needs and the feelings released by them (Rosenberg, 2009, p. 102).

The model of nonviolent communication assumes that every human being has needs.[1] Humans all share the wish to meet these needs but there are different strategies for trying to fulfill them. For example Person A enjoys loud music to relax whilst person B prefers silence. By living in a small house together their different strategies can lead to conflict, although both persons try to meet the same need for relaxation.

Feelings are always the expression of met or unmet needs (p. 69). For example, person B might get angry because he cannot fulfill his need for calmness. The loud music of person A is the activator of the anger but it is not its cause. Nonviolent communication strictly separates activators and cause. Cause of anger is always the person's own thoughts in the habits of mind of blame and denunciation (p. 164). An example which shows this aspect very clearly is as follows: Person A has got a date

1 cf. Rosenberg (2009) p. 216.

with person B in a restaurant. Person B is 30 minutes late. Person A could be angry thinking, "why can't he ever be punctual? Am I not important enough?" However, person A could instead think, "It's good to have a rest after that stressful day to relax and calm down until he arrives" or something else which does not activate anger.

Nonviolent communication does not mean that anger is something negative; in fact it is something valuable which can help people understand their needs. The point about anger is that everyone should take over the responsibility for their own feelings and should not blame others. Both blaming oneself and blaming someone else prevents nonviolent communication. People in Western societies are used to blame others for their feelings. This occurrence was underlined by the response to a question in survey 3. 48% of those questioned stated that there were people about whom or whose behavior they simply had to get angry.[1]

According to Gandhi, people in western societies are trained very early to be violent against themselves. They get taught to look at themselves as imperfect objects and therefore they judge themselves for everything that is not perfect. Almost everything and everyone appearing is judged right away. Gandhi pointed to the problem of looking at everything as black or white, right or wrong, you and I. Nonviolence seeks to understand people through real love instead of judging them and building a

---

1   cf. App. D.

Leadership for a Nonviolent Culture

wall between one another (Gandhi (2003) p. 23). Nonviolent communication tries to create awareness of these habits of mind and the ability to change them (Rosenberg (2009) p. 149-150).

The fundament of nonviolent communication is made of these five basic assumptions:

1. Humans are ready to cooperate when they can be sure, that their concerns get attention.
2. Needs are the motivation of every action. Every behavior serves the fulfilling of needs.
3. Every kind of criticism, attack and so on is the expression of unmet needs.
4. Every person has got remarkable resources and skills, which can be experienced by getting in touch with them empathically.
5. There are no hierarchies on the level of human relationships. There is equality amongst everybody.

Especially the fifth assumption can easily lead to confusion. According to Lindemann and Heim (2010), there is some kind of hierarchy in most organizations linked with roles, competences or just perspectives. They serve a certain intention, for example security and order. The phrase "no hierarchies on the level of human relationships" means that everyone's needs are taken equally seriously no matter which position (in an organization) a person has. By fulfilling needs at the cost of other people's needs unbalance occurs which stresses relationships and prevents voluntary cooperation (pp. 40-41).

Clear expression

There are four components of nonviolent communication to help people to express themselves clearly (Rosenberg, 2009, p. 25):[1]

Observation: Observation is what one sees, hears, remembers, imagines. It is a description and free of evaluation.

Feelings: Expression of the feelings that occur with the observation.

Needs: The feelings give hints to needs that are respected or maybe not respected.

Request: A clear request tells the opponent what he can do to contribute to his welfare and respect of his needs but it is not a demand.

These four steps help to prevent judgments or angry reactions, especially in difficult situations. It is important to express oneself clearly because misunderstandings are very common. This includes saying exactly what one wants the opponent to do, not what one does *not* want him to do. For example is it not clear enough to tell the partner that you do not want him to work that much when you want him to spend more time with you. He might think that you are only worried about his health and therefore want him to do something else other than working and as a consequence goes out with his mates at the weekend.

---

1 cf. Rosenberg (2009) p. 25.

Another point of unmistakable expression is that it has to be formulated in concrete action. For example, Person A asks his boss to be fairer. He, however, is of the opinion that he treats person A in a fairly. Person A could instead ask his boss to tell him privately in his office when he has made a mistake and not in front of colleagues, if that was the point person A wanted to get across to the boss as 'fair treatment'. The more people are aware of their own wishes and needs and are able to express them clearly, the more likely is their fulfillment (pp. 90-95). Even though it takes a lot longer to say something using the four steps of the model, in Survey 4, people agreed very much that nonviolent communication was very efficient because it can prevent misunderstandings and help to ease conflicts.[1]

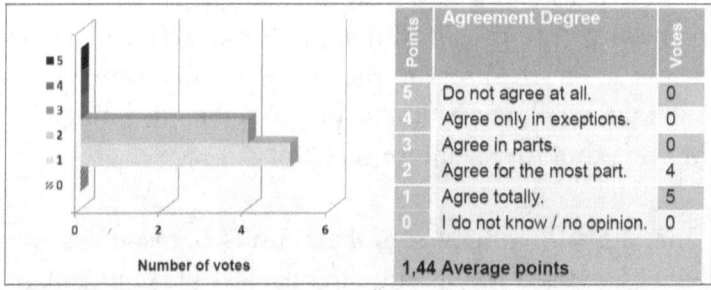

Fig. 17: Evaluation on statement "Nonviolent communication is efficient because it prevents misunderstandings and ease conflicts". Survey 4, app. E.

Another very important aspect of nonviolent communication is one's inner attitude. Nonviolent communication is not a means of getting people to work but the genuine attempt to understand the other person's needs. This attitude is essential in order to share real empathy.

1 cf. App. E.

The power of empathy

Rosenberg quotes Carl Rogers on the effect of empathy. Rogers describes that listening without judgment, without making the attempt to take over responsibility to form an understanding according to the listener's design, feels extraordinarily good. It helps to rediscover the world and the situation and seemingly insoluble problems suddenly become clear actions (p. 133). This concept has also been picked up by Michael Ende (1984) in his children's book Momo when he describes how much time Momo has to listen to everyone and how she does it without any judgment. Though Momo does not say a word when two arguing men come and tell her about their conflict, the conflict gets solved just because of Momo listening in a way that might be called 'empathically' (pp. 18-27). Although Momo is a fairytale, listeners to a reading of the story at the seminar in Heiligkreuztal were of the opinion that listening like Momo is not irrelevant for real life.[1]

Empathy for others sets those unused resources free which are used far too little in business life (Lindemann & Heim, 2010, p. 17) as the Gallup study on the Engagement index in Germany from 2008 demonstrates.[2]

As soon as people know about their needs and their tactics to meet them, they might want to substitute their (violent) tactics by ones which add to the nonviolent culture and the welfare of everyone. Therefore, nonviolent

1 cf. App. E.
2 cf. page 27.

communication in an organization can shape the organization's culture dramatically because it also makes people get in touch with their basic assumptions, their judgments and prejudices. On top of that, it can be used to help people realize what their needs really are and what truly motivates them.

Although there are many valuable aspects of nonviolent communication, it is not sufficient alone to create a nonviolent culture but is one of many facets. It is, for example, not enough to know and express one's own needs but it is also important to reflect whether needs have to be satisfied and, if so, with which strategies. Drosdek (2007) quotes Socrates who was of the opinion that not to need anything is something godly because someone who is happy with what he finds at any place will hardly fight a war. This is contrary to a person who has many needs and extensive ways of solving them (pp. 76-77).

The use of nonviolent communication in business

In business, the application of nonviolent communication is an important part of building a nonviolent culture and is also valuable for the improvement of performance. Many people during meetings complain about people talking at cross purposes. Often everyone just wants to promote their own viewpoint without being interested in listening to the arguments of others. The more clearly people express their concerns and what kind of resonance they expect, the more likely they are to get attention. It can be very helpful to let the opponent summarize what the person said in order to make sure that he understands it the way it was meant. Because people do not give the impression they want to their listeners, it makes sense to point out just why one considers repeating it to be important. In that way misunderstandings can be avoided and valuable time saved (p. 105). As demonstrated above, nonviolent communication can help to solve conflicts. It is also valuable to understand what truly motivates people and can improve motivation in the organization. Due to the possibilities of nonviolent communication, 8 out of 9 people in Survey 4 totally agreed or agreed on the whole that nonviolent communication was important for the economic success of a company.[1] As shown in the section *Global Productivity Study* on page 30ff., many employees at the investigated company (34% of those who filled in the questionnaire) thought that inefficient communication was one of the most important reasons for productivity loss in the company.

Criticism on nonviolent communication

Critical voices might wish to state that nonviolent communication is a nice model but not suitable for everyday use, especially not in business. This is probably a justifiable objection. Most people will not use it all the time, otherwise their spontaneity and individuality, to a certain extent, would get lost. Even when people do not use this model with every word they say, it does help one to change attitudes and to get in touch with the needs of oneself and of others. Especially in difficult situations,

1 cf. App. E.

Leadership for a Nonviolent Culture

when one is hurt by something another person has said, one can decide through which of the following 'four ears' he wants to receive the message (p.70).

Blaming ears to the outside:	Understanding-ears to the outside:
There is something wrong with the opponent, blame him for own anger.	What does the opponent feel and need? Understanding for the other person.
Blaming ears to the inside:	**Understanding-ears to the inside:**
There is something wrong with me. I am to blame for the other's anger guilt, shame or depression.	What do I feel and need? Understanding for myself.

Table 5: *The four kinds of receiving a message. (Based on Lindemann and Heim (2010) p. 101.)*

It can be necessary, that a hurt person first finds empathy towards himself (trying to get in touch with one's own needs in that moment) (p. 135) and trying to translate, for example, an attack into needs which the other person has.

For the translation of criticism or attacks, there is another four step model, similar to the first one (p. 213):

1. **Observation**: Observation is the questioning of oneself, what the opponent sees, hears, remembers, imagines. It is a description and free

of evaluation.

2. **Feelings**: Expression is the question, what feelings occur in the opponent with his observation.
3. **Needs**: Is about the needs which are hidden behind the feelings of the opponent.
4. **Request**: Is the question of what can be done to contribute to the welfare and respect of his needs but it is no demand.

Lindemann and Heim (2010) tell the story of a situation in business in which this model was used for better communication with a customer. Firstly, they demonstrate the situation when the persons are still caught in the judging 'blame-thinking' mindset. Then they show how the talk could have developed using nonviolent communication. This example demonstrates that nonviolent communication even works when only one conversational partner uses it. By knowing that beyond every criticism or attack there is the request for fulfillment of a need, one can become open to empathetically receiving a message without hearing personal criticism or blame (p. 149-150).

Another point about nonviolent communication which might be criticized is that because deep feelings and needs are brought up in nonviolent communication, applying the model can present a considerable challenge, especially whilst the concept is still new to people (p. 135). This is certainly a justifiable argument but building a nonviolent culture is no easy task and opportune conditions can be created to promote it. Nonviolent communication is easier for people in an environment where they feel safe and they know they can trust people. Trust is essential to ease the introduction of nonviolent communication.

Communication and trust

Covey (2003) states that the basis of effective communication is trust. Trust can never be built on organizational politics but only on trustworthiness (p.118). Covey explains the importance of trustworthiness, "When trust is high, people will still capture the meaning of the said whereas when trust is low, communication is difficult, exhausting and inefficient, because everything has to be explained complicatedly" (p. 18). The following graph shows the basic elements of which trustworthiness comprises. A trustworthy person truly cares for others, he keeps the commitments he makes and he has competency — both, professional and personal.

According to a question in Survey 1, 49% of the company staff had a trusting relation to their department and head managers based on the three points of caring, commitment and competency. 11% thought that there rarely was a trustful relationship. Criticisms were transparency of activity and commitment concerning statements. One person was of the opinion that openness, straightforwardness as well as contact to the employees should be improved.[1]

1 cf. App. B.

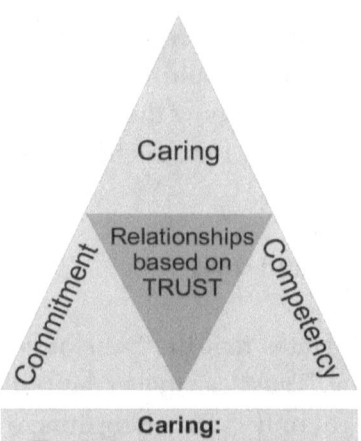

Fig. 18: Based on Egyptian (2009) p. 13, adapted from Blaine 1996.)

Gandhi was an extremely powerful leader because, due to his moral strength, he gained the love of millions of people. This is the very difference between Gandhi as a political leader and, for example, most of the US-presidents, who gained their power from military strength. Gandhi, on the contrary, gained people's trust because he was really concerned about his people and truly understood them. He assured himself of the miserable situation of the poor by taking their position and living as one of them before taking action (cf. Gandhi, 2003, p. 129). This behavior can easily be consigned into business life as the example of company RWE demonstrates. In terms of the initiation of culture change at RWE, people in leading positions left their desks for a day to work, for example, with technicians to get to know their viewpoint of work, for a better understanding of the culture. This was only one of many measures to change the culture at RWE (cf. Jumpertz, 2010, p. 58).

In the section entitled *A definition of nonviolence based on Gandhi's thinking* on page 55ff., Mahatma Gandhi's understanding of trust was discussed. Handy (1999), similar to Gandhi, is of the opinion that trust does not mean blind trust, stating that unbounded trust is unrealistic in practice. Handy sees trust as dependent on the experience with a particular person in a particular situation. He gives the example where a neighbor might be a great help in an emergency but yet cannot necessarily handle money reliably (p. 182).

The Learning Organization

According to Gandhi's understanding of (proactive) nonviolence, it is everybody's task to evolve the given talents and skills for the welfare of everyone, control one's own mind and to be constantly learning to create a nonviolent culture and lasting peace.[1] Therefore keeping people at continually learning and training their skills is an essential task of a leader who wants to create a nonviolent culture. An ideal implementation of organizational members constantly improving their abilities, Senge (1990) refers to as *The fifth discipline* or *The learning organization*.

---

1 cf. pp. 55ff.

In his book *The Fifth Discipline*, Senge (1990) quotes Arie de Geus, at that time head of planning for Royal Dutch Shell. According to de Geus, the only sustainable competitive advantage an organization might have in the future is its ability to learn faster than its competition. This statement also reveals the economic advantage or even future necessity of a learning organization.

At the heart of a learning organization's is what Senge calls *metanoia* which means a shift of mind. In Greek history it meant a fundamental shift or even the transcendence of mind, whereas in Christian tradition the word was used to express awakening shared intuition and a change of heart and was later translated as *repentance*. Senge uses the word *metanoia* to arrive at a deeper understanding of the term *learning*. He clearly points out that learning is not the same as 'taking in information'. Learning cannot be the same as taking in information, because after reading a book, for example on sports like paragliding, one will not automatically be able to paraglide. Just like metanoia, real learning is a shift of the mind. It is a kind of inner re-coordination, which will make people rediscover the world and their relationship to it over and over again. Learning enables people to create. Senge is of the opinion that everyone is naturally a learner because humans love to learn. There is a great longing for that kind of learning in humans. This longing is the basic meaning of a learning organization. Its purpose is not only to survive but to enhance its ability to actively create its future (pp. 4-14).

Creation of a learning organization

To create a learning organization a shared vision[1] and a new leadership style is necessary. According to Senge, the traditional leadership style was to give the employees "clear directions and well-intentioned manipulation to get people to work together towards common goals (p. 340)." This pushing employees into a certain direction by manipulating them is a form of violence because it impedes the evolvement of skills such as creativity.

Henri Fayol (1917) in Kirchler (2008) defines five tasks of a manager, which can be seen as the traditional tasks of a manager: To forecast and plan, to organize, to command, to coordinate and to control (p. 48).

These tasks very much sit alongside Senge's statement that traditional leadership was to 'give directions' and 'get people to work'. Such a style requires steep hierarchies and domination which do not fit into a learning organization.

After discussing several opinions on management and leadership, La Monica concludes that defined in terms of roles, management and leadership are totally different ideas. Whilst management is more bound to functions and organizational goals, a leader's role is rather to guide people in the organization (La Monica, 1944, p. 18).

---

1 cf section *Vision* page 70ff.

Senge (2009) defines three leadership types (pp. 341-357):

1. Leader as designer

The leader as designer creates the work field of the organization. His task is to create purpose, core values and a shared vision which leads to long-term thinking to enable people to learn as well as to support people in their learning process.

To visualize what influence the leader as designer has in an organization, Senge uses the picture of the ocean liner. The designer has more influence on its performance than for example the captain or navigator.

2. Leader as Steward

A steward shows people the coherence and interrelations of what they are doing and something bigger as the shared vision. They help people to understand how organizational needs evolve and how this fits in the big scheme of things which goes beyond the organization and affects society as a whole.

Covey (2003) calls a principle centered person a steward (p. 22). Principle-centered leadership is important for a learning organization as it helps to keep direction.

3. Leader as teacher

The leader as teacher helps others to understand reality at four different levels:
- Events
- Patterns of behavior
- Systemic structure

- Purpose story

The main task is to explain the answer to the question: "Where predominantly do they focus their organization's attention?"(p. 353). A *purpose story* helps identify people of an organization with a shared sense of purpose, giving them the explanation of the *why* mentioned in the section on vision on page 70ff.

This kind of leadership-understanding is completely different from traditional management and requires other skills of the leader.

Managers at our investigated company were of the opinion that Senge's three leadership models are applicable under certain circumstances. One person pointed out that the basis for these models are values and a vision which were not particularly present in the company. Another person stated that each model alone is not sufficient for leading. Maybe this opinion can also be traced back to the lack of vision. Although all agreed that these models might be applicable, nobody stated that they could imagine such a leadership style in the organization.[1]

The understanding of learning

To be truly able to learn, one has to understand one's own mental models. Mental models are subconscious assumptions and pictures of how people understand the world. They strongly influence the way humans think and act. They make people judge something they see or

1 cf. App. C.

which happens to them within seconds. A common example is that people get judged on the basis of what they are wearing. For example, somebody with a sports dress might be seen by person A as likeable and by person B as seedy and suspect. An important part of learning is to work with mental models. The understanding of one's own mental models affects all of a person's actions (p. 8).

Learning cannot be affected by pressure. Rudolf Wimmer, business manager of osb Wien Consulting GmbH states that the psychological strain, even during the crisis, was not strong enough to create real learning pressure. People will not challenge previous models and ask whether their performance will create real added value (Jumpertz and Bußmann, 2010, p. 55). The willingness to learn and to rethink known models requires a change of mind first. It is a process from the inside outwards which cannot be forced by external pressure.

Senge (1990) demonstrates the difficulty of team learning with the question: "How can a team of committed managers with individual IQs above 120 have a collective IQ of 63?" (p. 9). According to Senge, the discipline of team learning starts with *dialogue*, which means the free interchange of meaning within the group. Senge clearly suggests dialogue outside of a discussion. A discussion is an exchange of ideas in a winner-takes-all competition. Unless teams in an organization are able to learn, the organization will never itself learn (pp. 10-11). The improvement of communication in a company is essential for its learning capability.

Learning disability according to Senge

In his book *The Fifth Discipline*, Senge defines seven learning disabilities in organizations (pp. 17-26). With the help of questionnaires (Survey 1), the attempt was made to figure out whether there is a learning disability in the company complying with Senge's definition.[1]

Based on observation, the results of the survey were integrated into the table below. With respect to the four topics evaluated, on average there was a low learning disability in the company.

Next step in this research was to find out the reasons for these learning disabilities as well as their impact on the company results. This information is important if one is to create change towards a learning and nonviolent culture.

---

1 cf. App. I.

	No learning disability	Almost no learning disability	Low learning disability	Learning disability	No result
	+ +	+	-	- -	?
I am my position			X		
The enemy is out there		X			
The illusion of taking charge				X	
The fixation on events					X
The parable of the boiled frog		X			
The illusion of learning from experience					X
The myth of the management team					X
Sum		1	2	1	3

Fig. 19: Evaluation of learning disability investigated according to Senge's definition. cf. App. I.

In Survey 2, the result on employability at the company was that managers thought that people were not as employable as they should be.[2] Employability means that a person stays able to do a job due to his decision-making ability and responsibility as well as productive efficiency. This requires not only functional competences but also constant improvement of such qualities as the capacity for teamwork, competence in communication, responsibility and empathy (cf. Blancke, Roth and Schmid, 2000, p. 9).

There was the possibility for employees to participate in continuing education seminars in the organization in question. However, during the crisis almost no money was spent on continuing education. Managers received

2 cf. App. C.

training in professional skills but also soft skills like communication or team working ability. For 'normal' employees only functional seminars were offered. They were supposed to not only improve the employee's working skills but also promote personal development where feasible. One person criticized that there was little opportunity for promotion.[1] Functional improvement cannot be considered to be learning according to Senge's definition because there will be very little shift of mind. Functional improvement is generally about getting more knowledge on a certain subject. There was only a small amount of 'real learning' which would correlate to Senge's or even Handy's definition taking place in this organization. It would be necessary to start with a completely different understanding of learning.

Negative capability

Handy (1990) writes about *negative capability* as the means to handle complexity and unknown circumstances. He states that doubts and mistakes are something important because people learn from them. According to him, successful entrepreneurs "have on average nine failures for every success (p. 55)" but they count it down to experience. Learning starts with uncertainties, questions and doubts (pp. 54-56). Drosdek (2007) criticizes that many organizations still have a culture in which confession of ignorance is seen as a weakness. He is of the opinion that a sense of ignorance or lack of knowledge with important questions is necessary in order to spur the search for reasonable answers. The

1 cf. App. B.

overcoming of ignorance can come through knowledge from employees. It is important to ask specific questions in order to understand the knowledge of employees as well as the gaps in their knowledge. According to Drosdek, asking questions is part of leading. Drosdek points out an attitude of Socrates which was not to impose one's conviction on others but to help them to reach and use their own knowledge (pp. 52-54). This is an important point for promoting the ability to learn, whereas learning, as mentioned above, is essential for a nonviolent culture.

Learning to become nonviolent

Learning to become a nonviolent individual is an integral part of a learning organization with a nonviolent culture. This can start by learning to use nonviolent communication. It goes on by getting to know ones own mental models of judgement. A very difficult part to learn is not to judge. Krishnamurti (2001), an Indian philosopher, states that people can only learn when their mind gets completely still. The first step to learn is to accept not to know. The belief to know prevents learning because experiences and thoughts from previous events are projected into the actual situation. When this happens, a person cannot truly recognize 'what is'. Learning is similar to displaying empathy, just being there and experiencing 'what is', without judgment. According to Krishnamurti's thinking this is the highest form of intelligence. Another part of becoming more nonviolent is self-reflection. Zittlau tells that every day Gandhi used to reflect every single action. He demanded of himself to give account to everything he had done. This is a necessary measure to become nonviolent. It can be helpful to ponder on these five terms: Love, Respect, Understanding, Acceptance and Appreciation. To reflect every evening when one was loving, respectful, understanding, accepting and appreciating towards others during the day can help to integrate these principles naturally in everyday life. Learning to become nonviolent is a lifelong process and requires a lot of bravery, according to Gandhi.(cf. Gandhi, Merton and Kurlansky, 2007, p. 50).

The existence of a learning organization

Senge (1990) points out that it is not possible to declare to have become a learning organization because the more people know, the more they will realize how much they do not know. A learning organization is an ongoing process (p. 11). Drosdek (2007, p. 64) quotes Socrates again on that subject: "Only the one is wise who knows that he does not know it. It is no shame not to know but on the contrary very much so, when not wanting to learn"[1].

Conclusion about influencing culture through leadership

A nonviolent organizational culture can only evolve if the organization's leadership-style promotes it. A vision, principles and learning are essential for the creation of a

1 Translation from the German source: *Nur der ist weise, der weiß, dass er es nicht weiß. Es ist keine Schande nichts zu wissen, wohl aber, nichts lernen zu wollen.*

nonviolent culture. These parameters do not, however, only influence culture, the culture influences them as at the same time. For example, a culture which advances openness and responsibility allows good learning, whereas learning enables people to evolve the culture. It is a continuing interaction and leaders have the difficult task of having to work on both at the same time. This happens mainly by working on themselves and being an ideal, as demonstrated in the previous chapters.

Critical Summary

Ethics and Corporate Social Responsibility aspects are buzzwords in modern organizations. Many companies deck themselves with various titles and clothe themselves in social apparel yet the number of scandals in organizations has scarcely decreased. The problem is that a stance on social responsibility is demanded from outside of the organization's environment and from society. This work has argued that nonviolence must be accepted by organizations as a necessity in carrying out their task in their responsibility towards society. They are important factors in employee satisfaction and therefore for the success of the organization as a whole. However, unless leaders truly see the necessity for nonviolence, they will only try to whitewash. Morality and nonviolence require mental acceptance and cannot be enforced. Becoming nonviolent is a process from the inside out.

Another important part of this work was to point out the necessity of viewing a human as a whole and looking at his achievement with benevolence. By looking at the human as a whole, it is easier to recognize the resources and skills of every person which increases a person's satisfaction and an organization's performance.

In some chapters for example, the chapter on culture, fragmentation was criticized whilst at the same time mentioning that it can be necessary just to be able to embrace a topic at all.

This work only picked out a very small fragment of a very wide subject. Violence and nonviolence are facets which are present in all parts of human life but they are not the only ones. Therefore this topic represents only a small portion of an individual's life. Furthermore, only few aspects which are linked to violence and nonviolence have been considered. Religions for example, were not dealt with, despite the fact that they have influenced the acceptance or renunciation of violence in society for thousands of years in all cultures of the world.

Organizational culture is made of an unmanageable number of facets and influenced by various parameters. In fact, the subject of culture was also not exhaustively investigated. It can be concluded that leadership is one of the most important factors which influence an organization's culture and therefore it is essential for leaders to reflectively study to "become the change they want to see in the world."

Bibliography

Andrews, C.F. (2008) *Mahatma Gandhi's Ideas Including Selection from his writings.*

Alt, F. (2007) *Die Sonne schickt uns keine Rechnung*, 6th updated edition, München.

Die Finanzkrise 2008/2009, at: http://www.finanzkrise-2008.de/, 11.05.2010.

Balzert, H., Schäfer, C. Schröder M. and Kern, U. (2008) *Wissenschaftliches Arbeiten: Wissenschaft, Quellen, Artefakte, Organisation, Präsentation*, Witten.

Bancke, S., Roth, C. and Schmid, J. (2000) *Employability als Herausforderung für den Arbeitsmarkt – Auf dem Weg zur flexiblen Erwerbsgesellschaft – Eine Konzept- und Literaturstudie*; Stuttgart.

Behrend, M. (2006) *Deutliche Zunahme der Jugendgewalt*, at: http://www.welt.de/print-welt/article152866/ Deutliche_ Zunahme der_Jugendgruppengewalt.html, 11.05.2010.

Being, S. (2010) *Dschihadismus als Ersatzidentität*, at: http://www.wienerzeitung.at/DesktopDefault-

.aspx?TabID=4975&Alias=WZO&cob=489439, 11.05.2010.

Bihl, G. (1995) *Werteorientierte Personalarbeit*, München.

Bittelmeyer, A. (2010) Konzepte für die Karrieremitte in: *ManagerSeminare* Heft 143 (Februar 2010), Bonn, p. 60-64.

Bolzen, S. (2009) *Studie prognostiziert Tote durch Klimawandel*, at: http://www.welt.de/politik/article3824197/Studie-prognostiziert-Tote-durch-Klimawandel.html, 11.05.2010.

Bruhn, H.D. (2009) Der Traum vom lernenden Betrieb, in: Hölzle, P. *Personalmagazin*, 02/2009, Freiburg, p. 28-29.

Burke, E. at: http://www.quotationspage.com/quotes/ Edmund_Burke, 08.06.2010.

Bußmann, N. (2010) Wir müssen Dogmen überwinden. Interview mit EKS-Begründer Wolfgang Mewes, in: *ManagerSeminare* Heft 143 (02/2010), Bonn, p. 38-43.

Carnegie, D. (1999) *Sorge dich nicht – lebe! Die Kunst, zu einem von Ängsten und Aufregung befreiten Leben zu finden*, Augsburg.

Collins, J. et al (2009) *Die fünf entscheidenden Fragen des Managements*, Weinheim.

Cornelia, G. and Rosenstiel L. (2003) *Führung durch Motivation*, 3rd edition, München.

Covey, S. (2003) *Principle-Centered Leadership*, New York.

Dawtry, F. (1963) Delinquency and Non-Violence, in: Dunn (ed.) *A Search for Alternatives to War and Violence*, London, p. 27-31.

Deal, T. E. and Kennedy, A. A. (1982) *Corporate Cultures: the Rites and Rituals of Corporate Life*, New York.

Drosdek, A. (2007) *Sokrates für Manager: Eine Begegnung mit zeitloser Weisheit*, Frankfurt am Main.

Drucker, P. F. (1999) *The Drucker Foundation Self-Assesment Tool: Participant Work-book*, San Francisco.

Drucker, P. F. (2003) *The Essential Drucker. The Best of Sixty Years of Peter Drucker's Essential Writings on Management*, New York.

Egyptian, A. (2009) The Olive Branch teacher's guide: *Educational Supplement to the Youth Magazine of Seeds of Peace*, p. 13 in: http://www.seedsofpeace.org/files/TGWinter2009.pdf, 27.04.2010.

Ende, M. (1984) *Momo*, London.

Engelking, S. (2012) *The Beans and the Dreams, Part One – The Individual*, Tuningen.

Englander, E. K. (2003) *Understanding Violence*, second edition, Mahwah – New Jersey.

Festl, F. (2007) *20,000 Tote durch Terroranschläge*, at: http://www.focus.de/politik/ausland/jahresbericht_aid_55036.html, 11.05.2010.

Fritz, R. (1996) *Corporate Tides: the Inescapable Laws of*

Organizational Structure, San Francisco.

Frost, P. J. (1985) *Organizational Culture*, Newbury Park – California.

Frost, P. J. (1991) *Reframing Organizational Culture*, Newbury Park – California.

Gandhi, A. (2003) *Legacy of love: My Education in the Path of Non-Violence*, El Sobrante.

Gandhi, A. (1998) Lessons from Sevegram Ashram, in: Hesselbein, F. (ed.), Goldsmith, M. (ed.), Beckhard, R. (ed.) and Schubert, R.E. (ed.): *Community of the future*, San Francisco, p. 83-90.

Gandhi, M. K., Kurlansky, M. (preface) and Merton, T. (ed.)(2007) *Gandhi on Non-Violence: Selected Texts from and Mohandas K. Gandhi's Non-Violence in Peace and War*, New-York.

Gillett, N. (1963) Toynbee and History, in: Dunn (ed.): *A Search for Alternatives to Violence and War*, London, p. 8-12.

Gölzner, H. (2006) *Erfolg trotz Führung: das systemisch-integrative Führungsmodell; ein Ansatz zu Erhöhung der Arbeitsleistung im Unternehmen*, Wiesbaden.

Greenleaf, R. K., Beazley, H. (ed.), Beggs, J. (ed.) and Spears, L. C. (ed.) (2003) *The Servant-Leader Within: A Transformative Path*, Mahwah – New Jersey.

Greenleaf, R. K(1977) and Spears, L. C. (ed.) *Servant Leadership: A Journey into the Nature of Legitimate Power and Greatness*, New Jersey-USA.

Haller, W. (1990) *Die heilsame Alternative: Jesuanische Ethik in Wirtschaft und Politik*, 2nd edition, Wuppertal.

Handy, C. (1990) *The Age of Unreason*, Watertown.

Handy, C. (1999) *The Hungry Spirit. Beyond Capitalism: A Quest for Purpose in the Modern World*, New York.

Henke, D. (2009) *Studie: Deutsche reden nicht übers Geld*, at: http://www.geld-kompakt.de/2009/03/30/studie-deutsche-reden-nicht-ueber s-geld/, 19.06.2010.

Hitt, M., Ireland, D. and Hoskisson, R. (2008) *Strategic Management: Competitiveness and Globalization: Concepts & Cases*, 8th edition, Mason.

Hofstede, G. (1984) *Culture's Consequences: International Differences in Work-Related Values*, volume 5, Newbury Park.

Hofstede, G. (1991) *Culture's Consequences: Software of the Mind*, London.

Holler, I. (2005) *Trainingsbuch Gewaltfreie Kommunikation*, Paderborn.

Jumpertz, S. (2010) Die Energie der Bilder. Kulturentwicklung bei RWE, in: *ManagerSeminare*, Heft 143 (2/2010), Bonn, p. 56-58.

Jumpertz, S. and Bußmann, N. (2010) Aufbruch in die neue Gegenwart. Dritter Kongress X-Organisation, in: *ManagerSeminare*, Heft 143 (2/2010), Bonn, p. 52-55.

Kirchler, E. (2008) *Arbeits- und Organisationspsy-*

chologie, 2nd edition, Wien.

Kleine, J. (2009) *Engagement Index 2008, Kein Handschlag mehr als nötig*, at: http://www.focus.de/karriere/management/motivation/tid-13094/engagement-index-2008-kein-handschlag-mehr-als-noetig_aid_362023.html, 13.04.2010.

Kreuzhof, R. and Lambert, M. (2009) Skandal und Moral, in: *PERSONAL*, (11/2009), Düsseldorf, p. 6-8.

Krishnamurti, J. (2001) at: http://www.jkrishnamurti.de/jk_website/jk_ lehre/ jk_lehre_gemlern34.html, 22.06.2010.

La Monica, E. (1944) *Nursing Leadership and Management: An Experimental Approach*, Montery.

Lindemann, G. and Heim, V. (2010) *Erfolgsfaktor Menschlichkeit. Wertschätzend führen – wirksam kommunizieren*, Paderborn.

Lorenz, M. and Rohrschneider, U. (2007) *Praxishandbuch für Personalreferenten*, Frankfurt.

Lyberth, A. and Lüpke, G. (ed.) (2008) Das Eis in den Herzen schmelzen. Gespräch mit dem grönländischen Inuit-Schmanen, in: von Lüpke (ed.): *Altes Wissen für eine neue Zeit. Gespräche mit Heilern und Schamanen des 21. Jahrhunderts*, München, p. 58-80.

Marcic, D. (1997) *Managing with the Wisdom of Love. Uncovering Virtue in People and Organizations*, San Francisco.

Niebur, R. (2001) *Moral Man and Immoral Society: A Study In Ethics and Politics*, Louisville-Kentucky.

Pickartz, E. (2009) *Bringt die Finanzkrise die Globalisierung zum Stillstand?* at: http://www.wiwo.de/politik-weltwirtschaft/ bringt-die-finanzkrise-die-globalisierung-zum-stillstand-382649/, 08.04.2010.

Orth, G. *Jenseits von richtig und falsch – Fehler sind toll* - http://www.chs-mediation.de/pdf/jensits-von-richtig-und-falsch.pdf, 09.04.2010.

Proudfoot Consulting (2002) *Global Productivity Study*, at: http://enable06.myenable.com/fusion/apps/doc/ public/130/Productivity%20Study/Productivity_Study_ 2002_English_A4.pdf, 09.04.2010.

Rosenberg, M. (2009, 1) *Konflikte lösen durch gewaltfreie Kommunikation*, Freiburg.

Ruhlmann, W. at: http://www.allmusic.com/cg/amg.dll?p=amg&sql=33:3ifyxcwkldhe, 14.04.2010

Schein, E. (1995) *Unternehmenskultur: Ein Handbuch für Führungskräfte*, Frankfurt.

Schein, E. (2004) *Organizational Culture and Leadership*, third edition, Jossey Bass, San Francisco.

Schonfield, H. J. (2012) *The Politics of God*, Tuningen.

Schwartz, H. and Davis, S. (1981) Matching corporate culture and business strategy. *Organizational Dynamics*, Summer.

Senge, P. (1990) *The Fifth Discipline: The Art & Practice of The Learning Organization*, New-York.

KPMG AM (2009) *Survey on Conflict Costs in German and Swiss Companies by KPMG AG*, at: http://www.kpmg.de/ Themen/9249.htm, 14.04.2010.

Steyler Bank GmbH http://www.steylerbank.de/index.php? id=252, 22.04.2010.

Swaim, R. (2009) *The Strategic Drucker, Growth Strategies and Marketing Insights from The Work of Peter Drucker*, Singapore.

Theobald, K. (2009) Die wahren Werte, in: *Managermagazin* 12/2009, Hamburg, p. 162-166.

Wahl, P. (2010) *Der Atmosphäre ist Markt-Logik fremd* at: http://www.freitag.de/wochenthema/1009-der-atmosph-re-ist-markt-logik-fremd, 07.05.2010.

Warshaw, L. J. and Mager, J. (ed.) (1998) Violence in the workplace, in: Mager (ed.) *Encyclopaedia of Occupational Health and Safety*, 4th edition, volume 2, Danvers-Massachusetts (USA), chapter 51.2.

Weingart, M. (2004) *Fehler zeichnen uns aus. Transdiszipinäre Grundlagen zur Theorie und Produktivität des Fehlers in Schule und Arbeitswelt*, Bad Heilbrunn.

Wilber, K. (2001) *A theory of everything. An integral vision for business, politics, science and spirituality*, Boston.

Zittlau, J. (2003) *Gandhi für Manager*, Frankfurt am Main.

Appendices

Appendix A — The Work With Questionnaires

An important part of *Creating a nonviolent culture in a modern organization*, was the collection of data from practical experience. Therefore employees were questioned on many of the related subjects. According to Drosdek (2007, p. 53), who worked on the philosophy of Sokrates in management, the asking of questions is a very important part of leading.

Balzert et al (2008) pp. 56-57 give many reasons why the use of questionnaires is an adequate means of asking questions in such a work as this. Probably the most important is the anonymity of the respondents which enhances the straightforwardness of the answers. Additionally, people have time to think about the questions and the interviewer cannot influence the answers. Using questionnaires, many people can be questioned with relatively little effort and the examination of the data is quite easy. Amongst the problems encountered whilst carrying out a survey based on questionnaires are the rather short return rate which can distort the results. Another challenge is that people cannot enquire about ambiguities. During our survey on culture we noted that most people are not consciously aware of their habits and their assumptions.

Four surveys were made:

Survey 1: The first was to find out employee's attitudes regarding several company specific topics.

Survey 2: The second went deeper into management and leadership and was only addressed at department and head managers of of the researched organization.

Survey 3: The third questionnaire was on topics which were not company specific. This one was sent to people of all age groups by email.

Survey 4: The fourth questionnaire was about nonviolent communication and was given to the people at the seminar which the author held on 6 June 2010 at the Conference of the International Leadership and Business Society (ILBS) in Heiligkreuztal, Germany. Its purpose was to find out people's impression of nonviolent communication.

The researcher divided the topics into several questionnaires so that one questionnaire would not become too extensive. As soon as completion becomes too arduous, people are not motivated to do so.

Appendix B – Survey 1

Evaluation of Survey 1 based on 35 filled questionnaires (Return rate ca. 50%)

Why do you go to work?

For earning money.

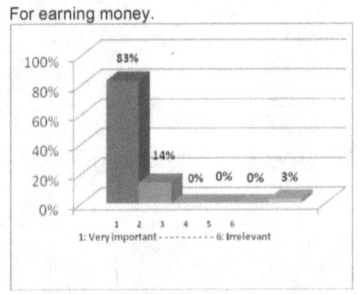

For building/selling machines.

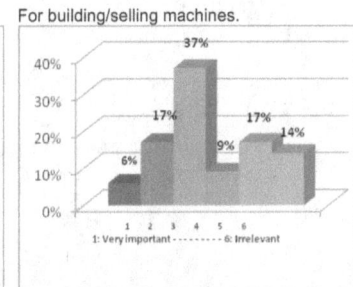

Because I am having fun at work.

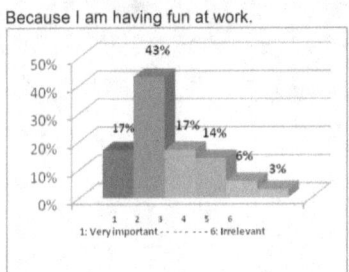

For being amongst people.

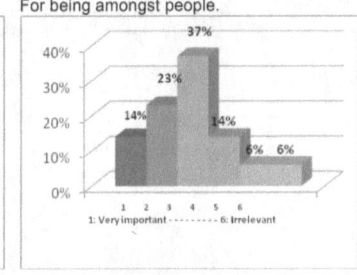

For having an occupation.

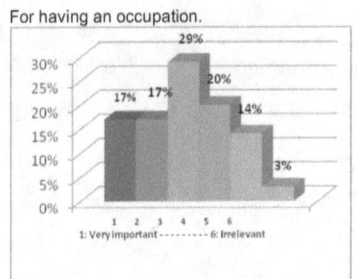

For self-actualization.

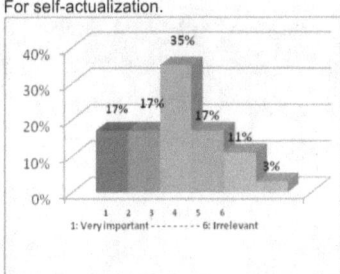

For living values.
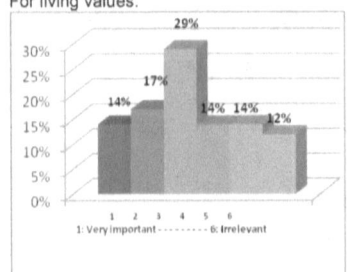

For serving the society.
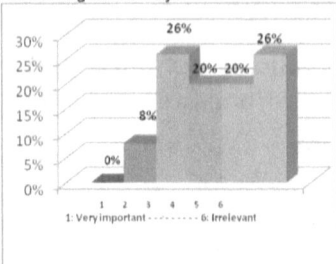

For temporarily having distance from my family.
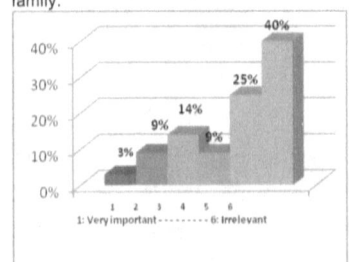

For keeping my social status.
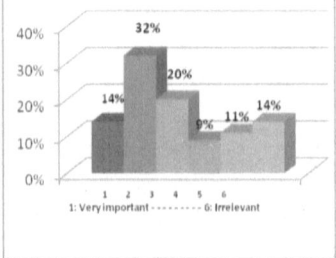

For being part of something greater (e.g. the company).
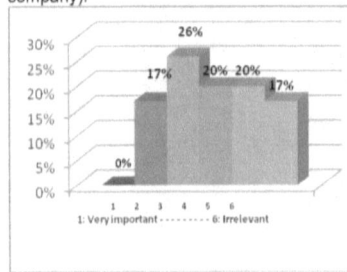

Appendices

How do you see yourself in your job?

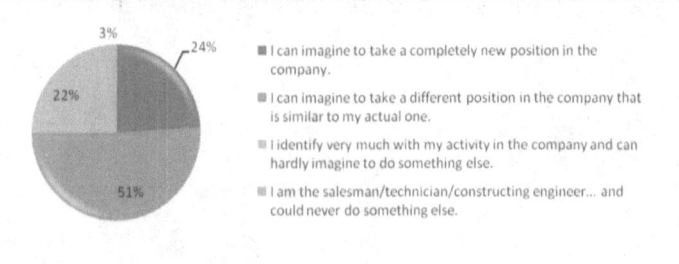

- I can imagine to take a completely new position in the company.
- I can imagine to take a different position in the company that is similar to my actual one.
- I identify very much with my activity in the company and can hardly imagine to do something else.
- I am the salesman/technician/constructing engineer... and could never do something else.

How do you see your responsibility?

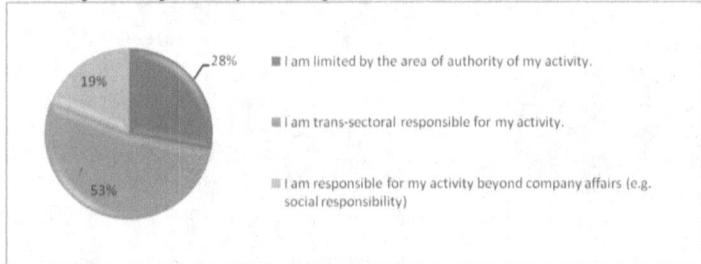

- I am limited by the area of authority of my activity.
- I am trans-sectoral responsible for my activity.
- I am responsible for my activity beyond company affairs (e.g. social responsibility)

How do you see the system* you operate in?
*System: Structural, cultural and other influencing occurrences within the company.

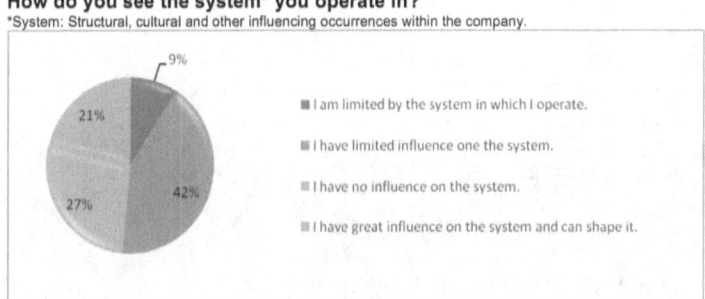

- I am limited by the system in which I operate.
- I have limited influence one the system.
- I have no influence on the system.
- I have great influence on the system and can shape it.

To what extend are you in the know about the interrelation of activities in the company?

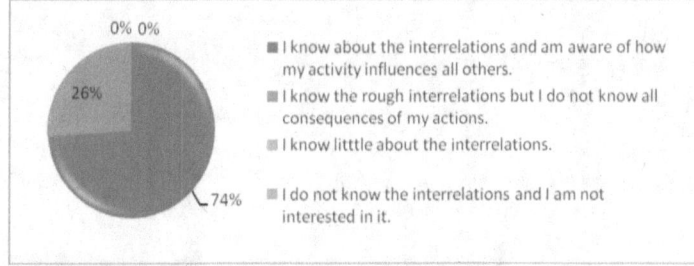

- I know about the interrelations and am aware of how my activity influences all others.
- I know the rough interrelations but I do not know all consequences of my actions.
- I know litttle about the interrelations.
- I do not know the interrelations and I am not interested in it.

148 Creating a Non Violent Culture in the Workplace

Does often go something wrong because of mistakes in other departments?

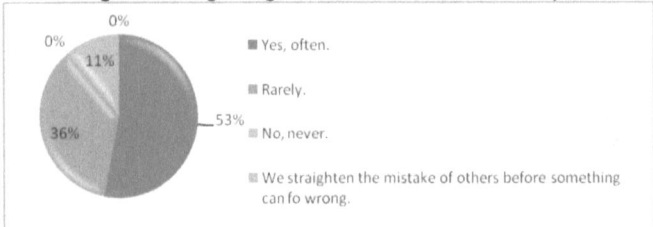

- Yes, often.
- Rarely.
- No, never.
- We straighten the mistake of others before something can fo wrong.

0%, 0%, 11%, 53%, 36%

How wide do you estimate the influence of external factors on the success of the company?

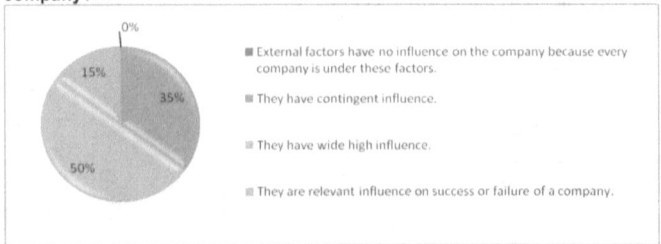

- External factors have no influence on the company because every company is under these factors.
- They have contingent influence.
- They have wide high influence.
- They are relevant influence on success or failure of a company.

0%, 15%, 35%, 50%

What has caused the firm crises with liquidity squeezes and personnel reductions in your company?

- It was exclusively caused by the worldwide economic crises.
- The worldwide crises and the banks are responsible.
- For some parts the economic crises, for some parts the crises was created internally.
- Th crises was homemade and was exclusively created internally.

3%, 3%, 8%, 86%

On what do you mainly concentrate your attention?

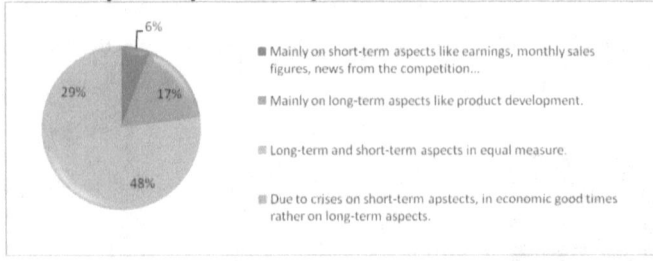

- Mainly on short-term aspects like earnings, monthly sales figures, news from the competition...
- Mainly on long-term aspects like product development.
- Long-term and short-term aspects in equal measure.
- Due to crises on short-term apstects, in economic good times rather on long-term aspects.

6%, 17%, 48%, 29%

Appendices

Do you recognize very little changes in your environment like for example a slight atmosphere change in society?

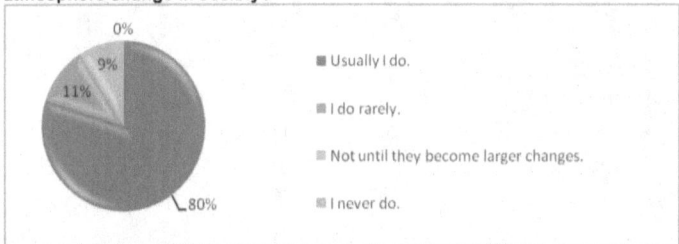

- Usually I do.
- I do rarely.
- Not until they become larger changes.
- I never do.

(0%, 9%, 11%, 80%)

Do you consider quick or slow changes as more threatening?

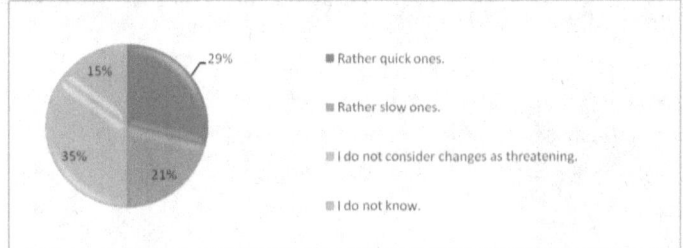

- Rather quick ones.
- Rather slow ones.
- I do not consider changes as threatening.
- I do not know.

(29%, 21%, 35%, 15%)

How do you make important decisions, of which you cannot foresee the consequences?

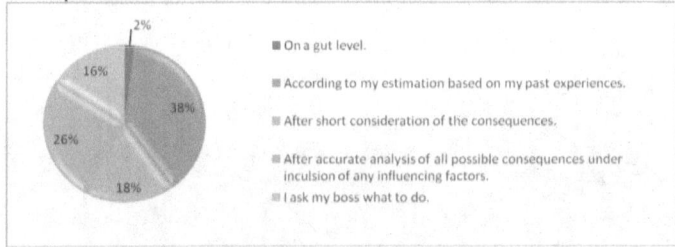

- On a gut level.
- According to my estimation based on my past experiences.
- After short consideration of the consequences.
- After accurate analysis of all possible consequences under inculsion of any influencing factors.
- I ask my boss what to do.

(2%, 38%, 18%, 26%, 16%)

How do you most commonly learn new tasks in the company?

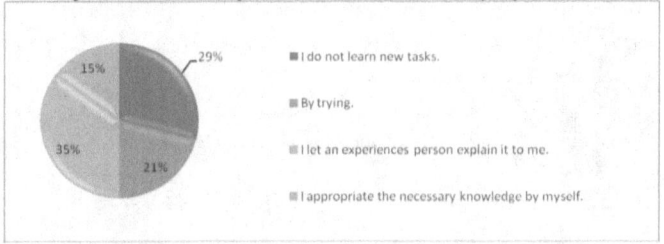

- I do not learn new tasks.
- By trying.
- I let an experiences person explain it to me.
- I appropriate the necessary knowledge by myself.

(29%, 21%, 35%, 15%)

How do you assess the working atmosphere in the company?

- Very good — 6%
- Predominantly good — 79%
- Rarely good — 9%
- Bad — 6%

Do you think that there exists a trustful liaison with the management (company and department management) based on following three points: Caring, commitment and competency (personnel and functional)?

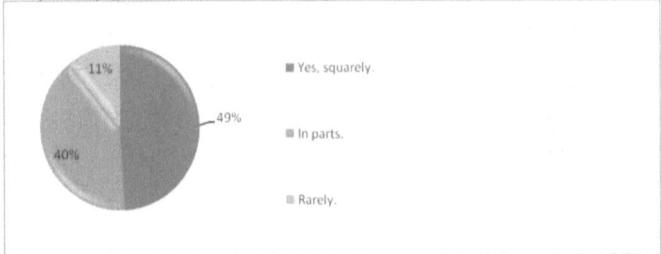

- Yes, squarely — 11%
- In parts — 49%
- Rarely — 40%

What causes in your opinion the greatest productivity loss in the company?

- Insufficient planning and control — 34%
- Inadequate management — 32%
- Poor working morale — 5%
- IT-related problems — 4%
- Inappropriate qualified workface — 6%
- Inefficient communication — 13%
- Others — 6%

How is your emotional engagement according to following definitions*?

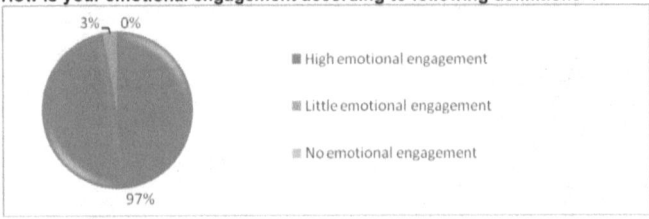

- High emotional engagement — 0%
- Little emotional engagement — 3%
- No emotional engagement — 97%

Appendices

How often are you confronted with conflicts in the company?

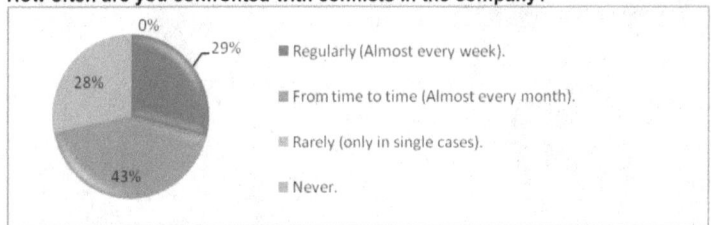

- Regularly (Almost every week).
- From time to time (Almost every month).
- Rarely (only in single cases).
- Never.

What kind of conflicts are they?

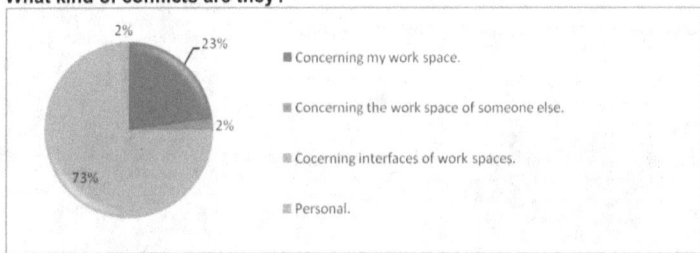

- Concerning my work space.
- Concerning the work space of someone else.
- Cocerning interfaces of work spaces.
- Personal.

How fast du you bring a conflict up?

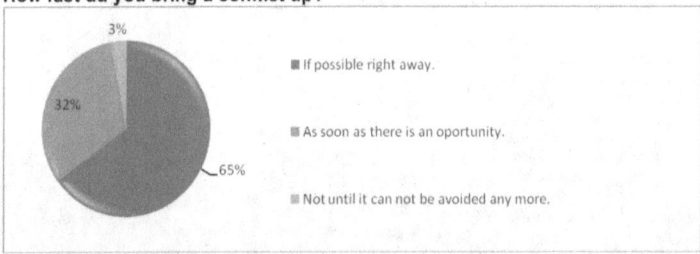

- If possible right away.
- As soon as there is an oportunity.
- Not until it can not be avoided any more.

Are the conflicts being solved to everybody's satisfaction without adding a third party?

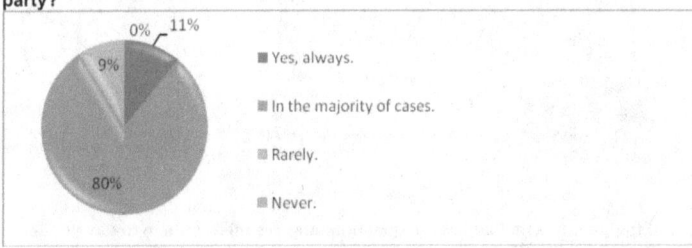

- Yes, always.
- In the majority of cases.
- Rarely.
- Never.

Do you know the content of the company philosophy (which is to be found e.g. on the company's website?

The last three questions were only for those who did not answer this question with "no."

Do you agree with the content of the philosophy?

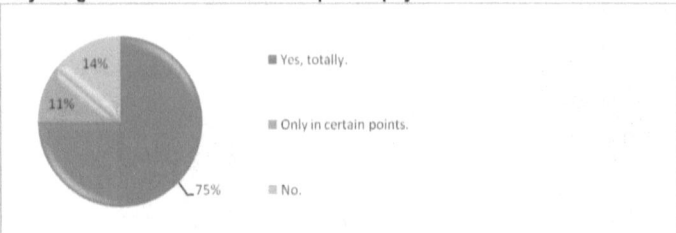

Do you think that a company's philosophy influences everyday work life?

Does the company philosophy influence your everyday work life?

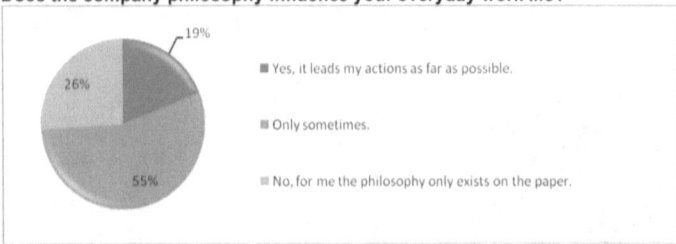

86% of the people who filled in the questionnaire are interested in the evaluation.

Appendix C – Survey 2

Evaluation of Survey 2, based on 4 questionnaires (Return rate ca. 57%)

How do you see the relation of harmony and conflicts in your team?

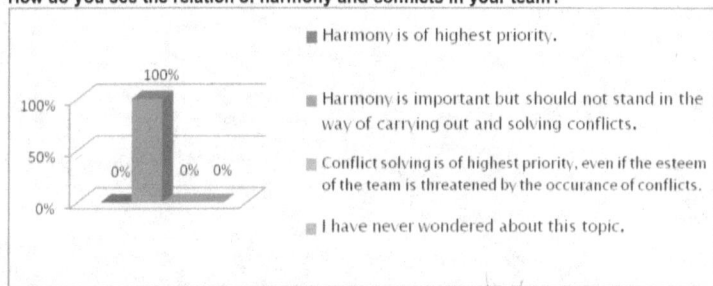

- Harmony is of highest priority.
- Harmony is important but should not stand in the way of carrying out and solving conflicts.
- Conflict solving is of highest priority, even if the esteem of the team is threatened by the occurance of conflicts.
- I have never wondered about this topic.

Is action in the company proactive?

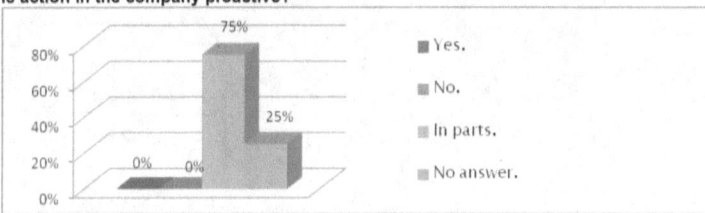

- Yes.
- No.
- In parts.
- No answer.

Are there certain principles that lead your business and everyday life?

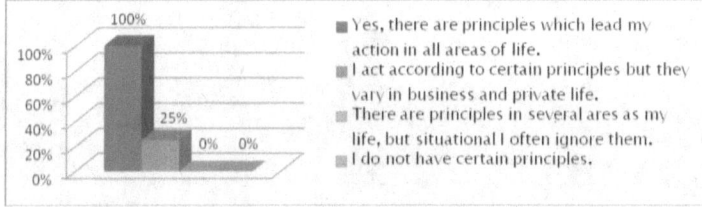

- Yes, there are principles which lead my action in all areas of life.
- I act according to certain principles but they vary in business and private life.
- There are principles in several ares as my life, but situational I often ignore them.
- I do not have certain principles.

As a leading person, how do you see your function as an ideal?

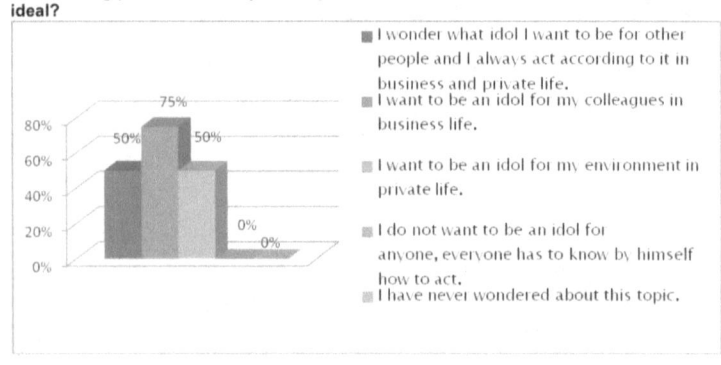

- I wonder what idol I want to be for other people and I always act according to it in business and private life.
- I want to be an idol for my colleagues in business life.
- I want to be an idol for my environment in private life.
- I do not want to be an idol for anyone, everyone has to know by himself how to act.
- I have never wondered about this topic.

Appraisal of employability in the company

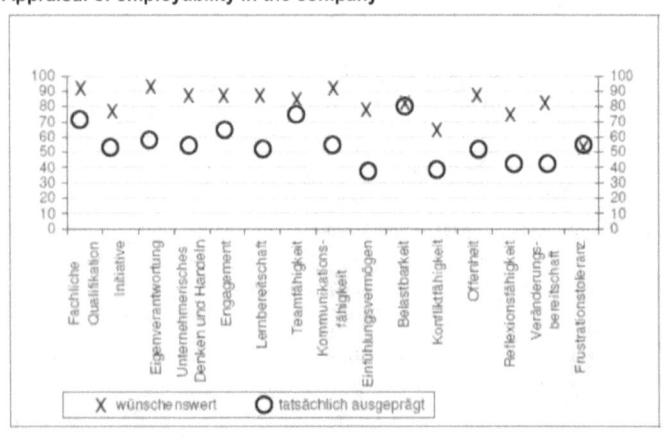

Appendix D – Survey 3

Evaluation of Survey 3, based on 27 filled questionnaires (Return rate ca. 40%)

Do you know for what purpose your deposit at a bank is used?

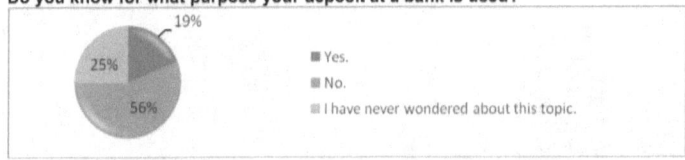

Does it matter to you, what your money is used for?

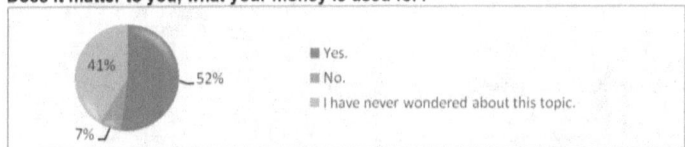

Would you choose a different deposit or bank if you knew that your money is invested into an organization whose activities you disapprove? (That might be producers of munitions, organizations participating in rainforest clearance, organizations violating human rights and so on.)

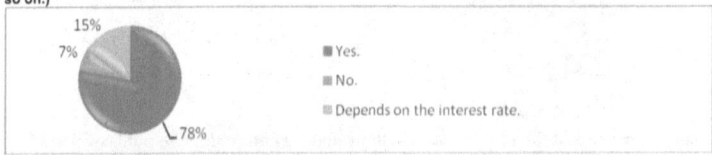

What do you think of the statement that talents are a gift and therefore everyone is a trustee of his talents and should develop and use them for the welfare of everyone.

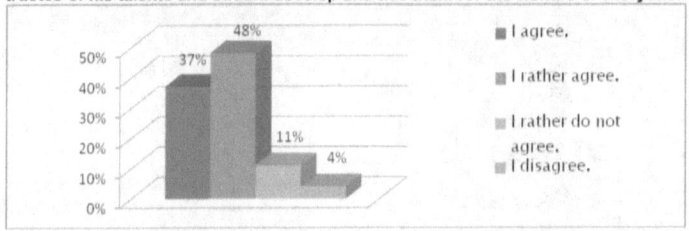

In the following questions, more than one answer could be checked. Each bar shows the percentage of people supporting an answer of all people who filling in the questionnaire.

How do you deal with saying the truth?

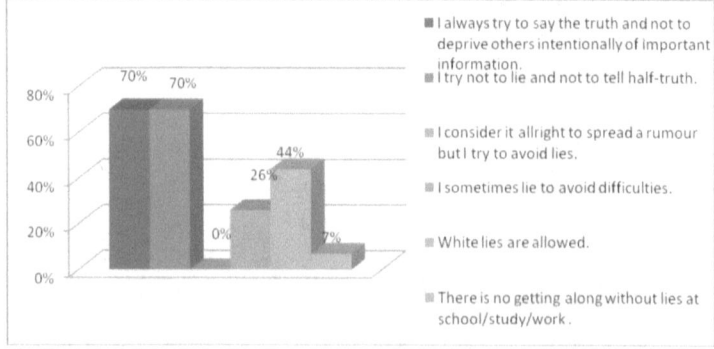

- I always try to say the truth and not to deprive others intentionally of important information.
- I try not to lie and not to tell half-truth.
- I consider it allright to spread a rumour but I try to avoid lies.
- I sometimes lie to avoid difficulties.
- White lies are allowed.
- There is no getting along without lies at school/study/work.

How do you deal with anger?

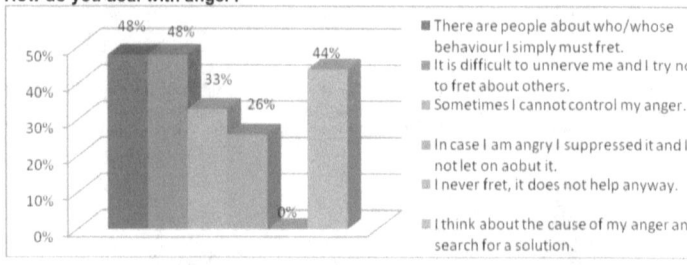

- There are people about who/whose behaviour I simply must fret.
- It is difficult to unnerve me and I try not to fret about others.
- Sometimes I cannot control my anger.
- In case I am angry I suppressed it and I do not let on aobut it.
- I never fret, it does not help anyway.
- I think about the cause of my anger and search for a solution.

How important is it for you that your actions make a contribution to public welfare?

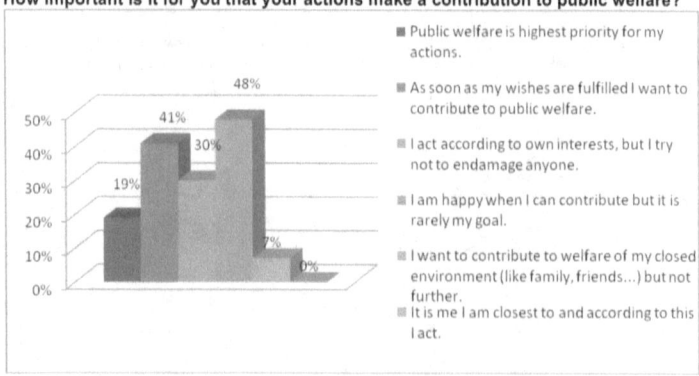

- Public welfare is highest priority for my actions.
- As soon as my wishes are fulfilled I want to contribute to public welfare.
- I act according to own interests, but I try not to endamage anyone.
- I am happy when I can contribute but it is rarely my goal.
- I want to contribute to welfare of my closed environment (like family, friends...) but not further.
- It is me I am closest to and according to this I act.

Appendices

What is your opinion on mistakes and malpractice? (Wie stehen Sie zu Fehlern und Fehlverhalten?)

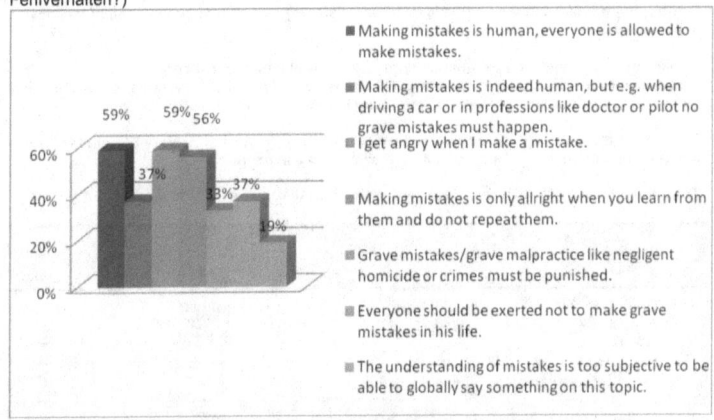

- Making mistakes is human, everyone is allowed to make mistakes.
- Making mistakes is indeed human, but e.g. when driving a car or in professions like doctor or pilot no grave mistakes must happen.
- I get angry when I make a mistake.
- Making mistakes is only allright when you learn from them and do not repeat them.
- Grave mistakes/grave malpractice like negligent homicide or crimes must be punished.
- Everyone should be exerted not to make grave mistakes in his life.
- The understanding of mistakes is too subjective to be able to globally say something on this topic.

Mahatma Gandhi named these seven points (see table) as cause of violence. Please chart in every rectangle a number from 0 to 5, to what extend you agree the statements concerning the single points.

- **0:** I do not know / no opinion
- **1:** Agree totally.
- **2:** Agree for the most part.
- **3:** Agree in parts.
- **4:** Agree only in exeptions.
- **5:** Do not agree at all.

	This point leads to violence							I avoid this point in my life					
	0	1	2	3	4	5	0	1	2	3	4	5
Wealth without work	7%	11%	26%	26%	22%	7%	8%	12%	20%	32%	8%	20%
Pleasure without conscience	4%	26%	44%	26%	0%	0%	8%	12%	28%	32%	20%	0%
Knowledge without character	11%	26%	41%	15%	7%	0%	28%	8%	44%	8%	4%	8%
Commerce without morality	0%	70%	26%	4%	0%	0%	4%	60%	28%	0%	4%	4%
Science without humanity	0%	56%	33%	7%	4%	0%	16%	52%	16%	4%	4%	8%
Worship without sacrifice	33%	7%	11%	15%	7%	26%	40%	8%	12%	8%	16%	16%
Politics without principle	4%	52%	33%	7%	4%	0%	24%	40%	24%	4%	4%	4%
Percentage of votes	0-25 %				25-50%				50-75%				75-100%

Dominance strategies in language

Below there are listed some linguistic dominance strategies which often are used in business or everyday life.

Please check the ones you experience regularly (several times a week) or use yourself (conscious or unconscious) in speaking. This does not only refer to situations at work but also on everyday life, for example with too late done house or flat share work.

Situation in this example: An employee says to his boss: „I am sorry, I cannot round the numbers up until midday. I simply cannot make it at the moment."

Taken from „Erfolgsfaktor Menschlichkeit" by Lindemann&Heim, published 2010, pages 32 + 33.

	Dominance Strategies	I experience this strategy regularly (several times a week)	I use this strategy myself.
1	To command, order, ask, expect, demand, require	44%	19%
2	To threaten, alert, either…or strategies	4%	4%
3	To moralize, preach	44%	26%
4	To give advices, give hasty solutions	48%	37%
5	To give lectures, disabuse, give facts	48%	48%
6	To reproach, judge, criticize judgmentally	15%	15%
7	To praise, adulate	22%	48%
8	To insult, make somebody look silly	7%	7%
9	To interpret, make a diagnosis, analyze	7%	22%
10	I have the feeling, that-sentences	15%	19%
11	To assign blame	15%	22%
12	To console, to evince sympathy, spare	11%	22%
13	To study, ask, interrogate, why-questions	48%	52%

14	Bossiness	19%	4%
15	To back out, distract, avoid	37%	30%
16	I cannot, I must – sentences	7%	11%
17	To hide behind responsibility, patronize, base oneself on an authority	22%	15%

Appendix E – Survey 4

1. Content of the workshop on nonviolent communication held on the 4th June 2010 in Heiligkreuztal, Germany. (Time. 1 ½ hours)

- Introduction with story of Marshall Rosenberg's life
- Assumptions the model of nonviolent communication is based upon
- Definition of needs
- Occurrence of feelings and their link to needs
- Strategies to fulfill needs
- Development of anger and conflicts
- Four steps of the model
- The meaning of empathy (including an abstract from the book „Momo")
- The four ears
- Practice of the model
- Discussion

2. General feedback on the workshop itself

This feedback was given verbally by the participants at the end of the workshop.

The personal feedback from the seminar was generally good. Those who already had some basic knowledge on nonviolent communication were of the opinion that a lot of useful content was communicated. One person who had heard of nonviolent communication for the first time wished to continue studying the subject and to take it deeper. Another idea from a listener was to compare this model with others concerning nonviolence and communication. For one person, for whom this model was new, mentioned that the topics brought up first made sense very late in the seminar, sometimes leading to confusion. He suggested illustrating the single topics during presentation from time to time.

Appendices

Points	Agreement Degree
5	Do not agree at all.
4	Agree only in exeptions.
3	Agree in parts.
2	Agree for the most part.
1	Agree totally.
0	I do not know / no opinion.

German language is very violent.

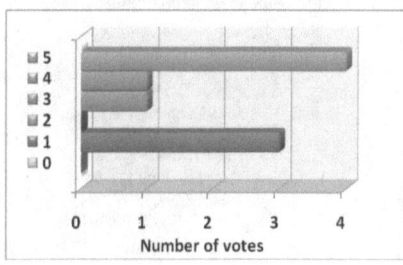

Points	Agreement Degree	Votes
5	Do not agree at all.	4
4	Agree only in exeptions.	1
3	Agree in parts.	1
2	Agree for the most part.	0
1	Agree totally.	3
0	I do not know / no opinion.	0
3,33 Average points		

Language is instrumentally responsible for the emergence of violence.

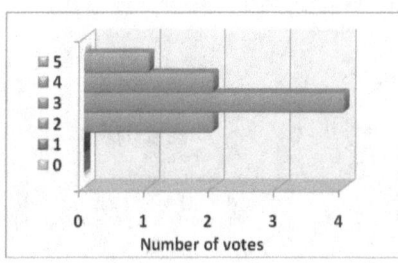

Points	Agreement Degree	Votes
5	Do not agree at all.	1
4	Agree only in exeptions.	2
3	Agree in parts.	4
2	Agree for the most part.	2
1	Agree totally.	0
0	I do not know / no opinion.	0
3,22 Average points		

164 Creating a Non Violent Culture in the Workplace

Nonviolent communication plays an important role in prevention of violence in society.

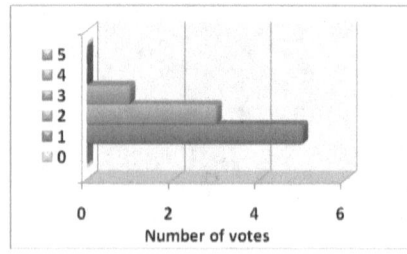

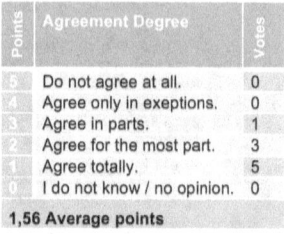

Points	Agreement Degree	Votes
5	Do not agree at all.	0
4	Agree only in exeptions.	0
3	Agree in parts.	1
2	Agree for the most part.	3
1	Agree totally.	5
0	I do not know / no opinion.	0

1,56 Average points

Nonviolent communication is efficient because it prevents misunderstandings and ease conflicts.

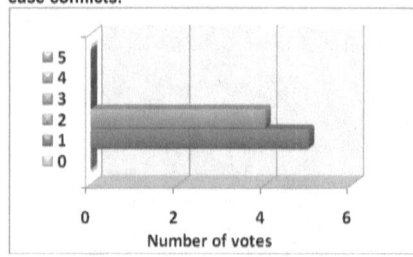

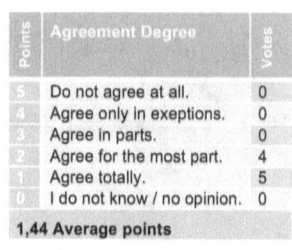

Points	Agreement Degree	Votes
5	Do not agree at all.	0
4	Agree only in exeptions.	0
3	Agree in parts.	0
2	Agree for the most part.	4
1	Agree totally.	5
0	I do not know / no opinion.	0

1,44 Average points

Nonviolent communication is important for the economic success of a company.

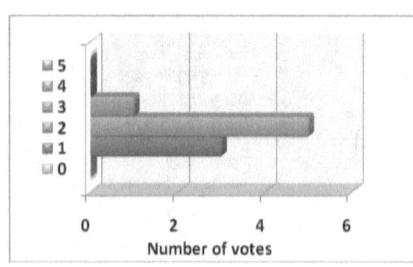

Points	Agreement Degree	Votes
5	Do not agree at all.	0
4	Agree only in exeptions.	0
3	Agree in parts.	1
2	Agree for the most part.	5
1	Agree totally.	3
0	I do not know / no opinion.	0

1,78 Average points

Appendices

Nonviolent communication is adequate for everyday contact with each other.

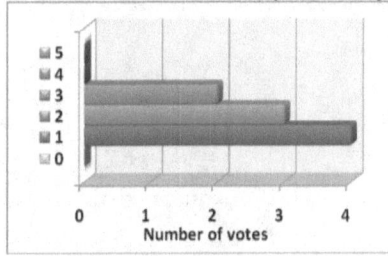

Points	Agreement Degree	Votes
5	Do not agree at all.	0
4	Agree only in exeptions.	0
3	Agree in parts.	2
2	Agree for the most part.	3
1	Agree totally.	4
0	I do not know / no opinion.	0

1,78 Average points

Nonviolent communication can be learned by everyone

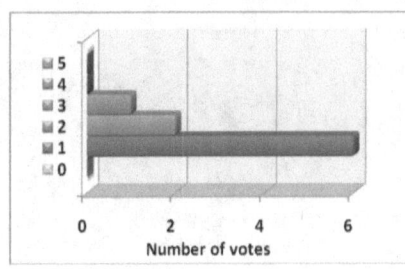

Points	Agreement Degree	Votes
5	Do not agree at all.	0
4	Agree only in exeptions.	0
3	Agree in parts.	1
2	Agree for the most part.	2
1	Agree totally.	6
0	I do not know / no opinion.	0

1,44 Average points

To give real empathy is learnable.

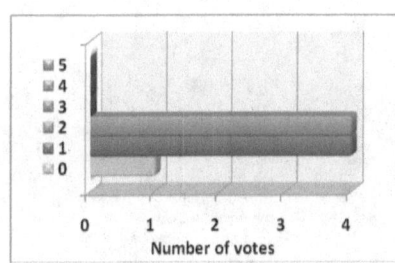

Points	Agreement Degree	Votes
5	Do not agree at all.	0
4	Agree only in exeptions.	0
3	Agree in parts.	0
2	Agree for the most part.	4
1	Agree totally.	4
0	I do not know / no opinion.	1

1,5 Average points*

*the vote "0: I do not know" is not counted

166   *Creating a Non Violent Culture in the Workplace*

To be able to listen like Momo only works in fairytales and is of no interest for everyday life.

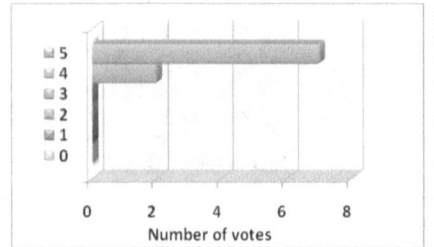

I want to try to use nonviolent communication in difficult situations.

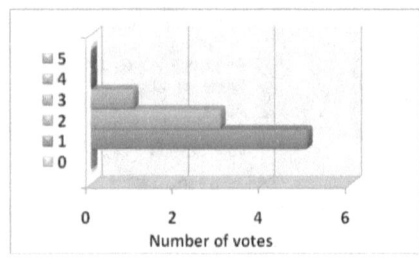

I want to try to integrate nonviolent communication in my everyday life.

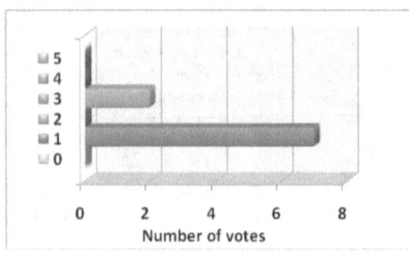

Appendices

Nonviolent communication can help to better get to know the own needs.

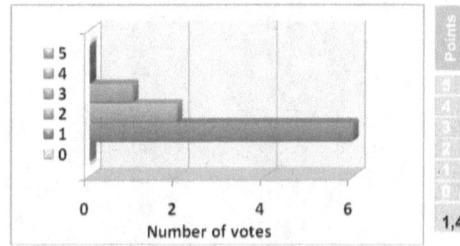

Points	Agreement Degree	Votes
5	Do not agree at all.	0
4	Agree only in exeptions.	0
3	Agree in parts.	1
2	Agree for the most part.	2
1	Agree totally.	6
0	I do not know / no opinion.	0

1,44 Average points

I can imagine participating in a seminar on nonviolent communication.

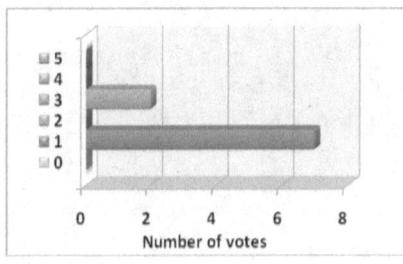

Points	Agreement Degree	Votes
5	Do not agree at all.	0
4	Agree only in exeptions.	0
3	Agree in parts.	2
2	Agree for the most part.	0
1	Agree totally.	7
0	I do not know / no opinion.	0

1,44 Average points

Appendix F — Principles of the Mondcivitan Republic

The Mondcivitan Republic is a body which understands itself as a servant nation and which does not claim land or power. Its purpose and highest priority is to serve mankind. It has got members from all parts of the world which represent the world's population. It has got strong principles as the basis of its action for peace and justice[1]:

No-one is an Enemy

No-one is a Foreigner

Service to All

Complete Impartiality

Work for Peace

True Democracy

Equity and Justice

Principles (Detailed Version, Schonfield, 2012, pp. 226-227):

1. The Mondcivitan Republic acknowledges none as enemies, no matter what they may do; for to admit the existence of an enemy is to create a barrier, darkening understanding, breeding hatred, and giving encouragement and license to cruelty and inhumanity.

1 http://www.schonfield.org/

2. The Mondcivitan Republic recognizes none as foreigners, or of a lower dignity, since all belong to the same human race. There shall be identical treatment of those outside the Commonwealth as of those within it, treatment that is founded on reverence for the human personality.
3. The Mondcivitan Republic shall ever promote and actively assist measures for the welfare and equitable unification of mankind, and shall at all times respond to the extent of its ability to calls for aid in emergency or catastrophe.
4. Neither the Commonwealth, nor any of its citizens, shall under any circumstances engage in war or in preparation for war, or in aggression, oppression, or willful misrepresentation. The Mondcivitan Republic shall ever hold itself free from all alliances, agreements and contractual obligations, whether open or secret, which can have the effect of favoring any group, party, section, or state, or any interests whatever, to the hurt or detriment of any others.
5. The Mondcivitan Republic shall study to be impartial in all its relations and judgments, and shall labour in the cause of mediation and reconciliation.
6. The character of the Commonwealth is democratic and cooperative, based on mutual service and respect, holding all men in honor in public and private.

7. In its government and internal economy the Mondcivitan Republic shall continually seek to cultivate and display those standards of conduct which are equitable and just.

	What is meant	Action in the company
No-one is an Enemy	No-one is an Enemy, no matter what he or she does. To admit the existence of an enemy is to create a barrier, darkening understanding, breeding hatred, and giving power and license to cruelty and inhumanity.	No-on is an enemy - competitors are no enemies! They motivate us to work more efficiently, create real benefit for customers, develop new markets... Thinking bad of others and complaining creates bad atmosphere and blocks creativity and freedom in thinking.
No-one is a Foreigner	To recognize no-one as a foreigner, or of lower dignity, since all belong to the same human race determining to treat all, whether fellows or not, in a way which is founded on reverence for the human personality.	No discrimination of race, religion, social classes... To treat everybody as a response to their personality. Learn about other cultures to establish respect and understanding and avoid misunderstandings. Use cultural differences for new ideas and innovation.

Appendices

	What is meant	Action in the company
Service to all	Ever promoting and actively assisting all measures which are the welfare and equitable unification of mankind and at all times responding to the extent of ones ability to any call for aid in an emergency, catastrophe or apparent need.	Might be seen as the key principle of leadership and maybe also the hardest one for the leader: Service to customers, employees, suppliers, shareholders and owners but also service for environment and help in case of social needs and catastrophes.
Com-plete Impartiality	Not to engage in aggression, oppression or willful misrepresentation to avoid all such behavior. To hold oneself free of al alliances, agreements and contractual obligations, which can have the effect of favoring anyone, or any interests whatever, to hurt or detriment others.	No aggression, no oppression, which includes for example production in low wage countries where people are oppressed, no willful misrepresentation, no agreements at the costs f others like price cartels. Truthful and aggression-less behavior as objective as possible at all terms.

	What is meant	**Action in the company**
Work for peace	Studying to be impartial and humane in all relationships and judgments and laboring in the cause of mediation and reconciliation.	Being open, friendly, criticize openly face to face, settle disagreements and reconcile after an argument.
True Democracy	Working in the interest of true democracy in a cooperative spirit, based on mutual service and respect, holding all persons in honor in public and private.	Cooperative decision-making, not on costs of the minority. It will help decisions being carried out by all organization. Holding people in honor, also when the phone is hung up. No cheating the customer, serve his needs.
Equity and Justice	Continually seeking to cultivate and display those standards of conduct, both in public and private life, which are equitable and just.	Discuss openly feelings of not being treated equitably because such dissatisfaction amongst employees is strong de-motivator.

Table 6: Principles of the Mondcivitan Republic. (Based on Schonfield (2012) pp. 226-227.

Appendix G - Documentation of the Researcher's Experiences

Documentation 1: Experience with lies in the company

From 22.03.2010 until 02.07.2010 the researcher worked in the sales department of the company. Part of her and her colleagues' (sales assistants') work was to answer calls on the main switchboard number. Especially cold-callers who wanted to talk to the head manager were told that he was not available, even if this was not the case. This happened for example on 23.06.2010 when a gentleman had called several times.

Documentation 2: Experience on learning from mistakes

From 22.06.2009 until 23.12.2009 the researcher worked in the export department. Due to short-time working of many colleagues, on average three times a week, she often was on her own organizing the shipment of spare parts and machines to the whole world. One time she made the mistake of sending a small spare parts package to Turkey without filling in an A.TR, a document required by Turkish customs authorities. Although this document was missing, the spare parts reached their destination without delay. The export coordinator had already realized that customs are not so strict concerning required documentation as long as the value of the shipment is low. After realizing what had been a mistake in

September 2009, he decided not to fill in an A.TR for low value shipments in future to save effort.

Documentation 3: Experience with judgements in the German language

The authoress read Marshall Rosenberg's book *Gewaltfreie Kommunikation* in January 2010. Afterwards she tried to use it several times in her everyday life. She felt that she was not very successful in doing so but realized how everything is judged immediately on almost anything one says. On 26th and 27th March 2010 the authoress attended a seminar on nonviolent communication at *Knoten Lösen* in Reutlingen. Afterwards she became even more aware of people's judging habits of mind and language including her own. This was present in private life as well as in business life.

Documentation 4: Discussion with the company's human resource manager

First meeting: 06.05.2010 on the company premises

Second meeting: 09.06.2010 on the company premises

The topics which were discussed concerned the company's culture. The application of Schein's, Deal and Kenedy's and Hofstede's cultural models to the company was discussed as well as the attempt of leading persons to influence the culture. Besides structural factors, the philosophy and handling of mistakes were topics of the meetings. Final discussion points were motivational methods and the understanding of learning within the company.

Documentation 5: A colleague quits

During this period, an employee gave notice. When asked about the reason, she said that she had asked for pay rise a few times. At that time she did not receive a higher salary due to the difficult time the company was having during the crisis. Then she applied for a different job and got an offer with a much higher salary, which she accepted No further information on the subject is available.

Documentation 6: Experience with dissatisfaction due to feeling unfairly treated

The author's husband (who did not work at the company in question) had been quite satisfied with his salary for the job he was doing. In February 2010 he accidentally found a list with the salary of all people in the company. He felt that he was doing a lot more work than one of his colleagues who received almost twice his salary. Since that day he is discontented with his salary because he is of the opinion that he does not earn enough.

Appendix I: Survey on learning disability according to Senge's definition

In his book "the fifth discipline", Senge (1990) defines seven learning disabilities in organizations (p. 17-26). With the help of the above listed questionnaire (Survey 1), an attempt was made to discover whether there is a learning disability in the company according to Senge's definition.

1. I am my position

After a failed try to retrain employees of a steel company in 1980, psychologists discovered that it was not working because people could not identify with a new job. Their identity was dependent on the position. Opinions like "I am the operator" were expressed. Those people saw their responsibility as being bound to the job and hence limited, because they felt themselves to be part of a system over which they have no influence.

This occurrence shows the importance of identification with the whole company. If people cannot identify with the organization, its vision and principles, they seek other ways of identification such as their work. Only 24% of the questioned in survey 1 answered that they could imagine taking a completely different position in the company. But 51% stated that they could do a different job that is similar to their actual one. 25% could hardly or hardly not imagine doing a different task.

With regard to responsibility, 53% of the questioned people felt responsible for cross boundary concerns too and 19% even felt responsible for concerns beyond company affairs. Most of the people in the company in question (70%) thought that they had a limited or no influence on the system in which they operated . All of those questioned were of the opinion that they at least knew in general how their actions influenced others[1]. It would appear that the learning disability "I am my position" appears at the company concerned but not to such a high degree as described by Senge.

2. The enemy is out there

It is in human nature to find someone or something that is to blame when something goes wrong. In organizations, this search for a culprit can be external or internal, for example between departments. Manufacturing blames engineering, engineering blames construction department and so on. External culprits can be the competition, the state, the "bad circumstances" and a crisis. It does not mean that these factors do not have influence on the result but they are not the only reasons for it. In the company we researched, many people were of the opinion that external factors had a great influence on the company success (50%) and some (15%) were of the opinion that they were even decisively responsible for it. On top of that 53% stated that in their department something often went wrong as a result of mistakes in other departments. It is hard to judge whether this was the case or whether it was people's tendency to name a cul-

1 cf. App. B.

prit. On the contrary, however, 86% of the employees were of the opinion that the crisis in the company was a result of both internal and external factors. 8% of them even thought that the crisis was exclusively created internally[1]. We can therefore conclude that there is no apparent strong learning disability concerning "the enemy is out there."

3. The illusion of taking charge

Senge describes how many organizations claim to be proactive which means taking aggressive action against possible enemies before a problem can develop to a crisis. This, according to Senge, is hidden reactiveness. Real pro-activeness is a way of thinking, namely the realization of how one contributes to one's own problems. Questioning company managers on proactive action, nobody defined it as a realization of one's contribution to one's own problems. 75% of those who answered the questionnaire stated that in some departments there was proactive action in the company, whilst 25% did not give an opinion[2]. The conclusion seems to be that there is rarely proactive action in the company, which accords with Senge's definition.

4. The fixation on events

Life is often seen as a series of consecutive events. This fact comes to light when children explain why they fight. "I hit him because he took my ball", "I only took it

1   cf. App. B.
2   cf. App. C.

because she would not let me play with the airplane", "I did not let him play with the airplane, because last time he broke the propeller." Just like children, adults tend to think that there is an obvious cause for every happening. Organizations often are only concerned with events, such as last month's sales or the new competition just announced. By focusing on events, learning to create is retarded, which is necessary for long-term processes like product design, environmental care and so on. On this topic, results from the survey have limited informative value because only one question was asked, namely what people focus on more, short-term or long-term events. 48% of the people stated that their long and short-term view was balanced. 29% stated that due to the crisis they focused on short-term events but usually they tended to concentrate on the long-term[1]. No conclusions on this learning disability can be arrived at on the basis of these results.

5. The parable of the boiled frog

The parable of the "boiled frog" is also relevant to a well-known problem in economics. If one puts a frog in boiled water, it will try to jump out immediately. But if it gets into room temperature water without being scared, it will stay. By raising the temperature slowly, it will first enjoy the rise of temperature but as it gets over 70 or 80 centigrade, it gets too groggy to climb out of the pot. The frog will sit there until it dies. Although gradual processes often pose the greatest threats they are often ignored or even not realized. To be able to react to

1   cf. App. B.

slow gradual processes, it is essential to slow down and pay attention to subtle as well as to dramatic occurrences. Answering the question whether they considered slow or fast change as more threatening, 35% of those asked did not think of change as threatening whereas the number of people who felt threatened by change was quite balanced (slow 29%, fast 21%). 15% did not know what to answer. Maybe they had never thought about this topic. 80% of the people were of the opinion that they noticed even the smallest changes in their environment[1]. According to this result, there is no strong learning disability which would correlate with "the boiled frog" syndrome. However, here again, it is not possible to arrive at final conclusions. More clarity could have perhaps been attained if the question of how people react to small changes in their environment or if they react at all had been asked.

6. The delusion of learning from experience

People get the best learning effect through learning from direct experience[2]. This is a dilemma because often the consequences of important decisions never get known. As soon as people reach their "learning horizon" and cannot observe the consequences of their actions anymore, the concept of learning from experience is not appropriate. When the consequences of actions are so far in the future or the system is too complex to understand, one cannot see the consequences of one's actions anymore. Then it gets impossible to learn from experience

---

1 cf. App. B.
2 cf. Bruhn and Hölzle (2009) p. 29.

due to the fact that the person does not experience the outcome of his actions any more. There are decisions made in organizations which have consequences for many years. For example the appointment of a new person in a leading position will shape the climate and culture of the organization for years. 38% of people at the company investigated stated that they made decisions for which they could not foresee the consequences based on past experiences. 18% thought briefly about possible consequences and 26% tried to include all possible influencing factors when considering consequences. 16% asked their boss when they were not sure how to decide. Many people deliberated on the possible consequences of their actions. When it came to the question of how to learn new tasks in the company, 31% of the people who answered the questionnaire stated that they learnt new tasks through experimentation. 46% answered that they let an experienced person explain it to them and that they thus acquired the necessary knowledge. To figure out the degree of learning disability "the illusion of learning from experience" at least one other question would have been necessary. The question that should have been asked in this context is whether people often have to make decisions about issues on which they do not get to know the outcome or do they first get to know about the outcome, very much later. This question was omitted from the questionnaire but it would have provided further insights on this topic.

7. The myth of the management team

The management team in an organization has experts and the collection of intelligence is supposed to solve all dilemmas and disabilities. However, very often these teams are busy avoiding conflict in order to maintain appearances or break down under the pressure of issues which prove to be too complex. One reason for the occurrence of such behavior can be due to the inherency of the organizational culture when the solving of urgent problems leads to the achievement of a higher status than introduction of difficult topics which concern organizational policies. People in such a situation assume a high degree of professionalism in blocking the new understanding. This aspect can become a threat for the organization. 100% of the managers stated that harmony in their team is important but should not prevent conflicts from being solved. Nobody stated that conflict-solving was the highest priority in their team or whether conflict-solving threatened their esteem[1]. This result on its own is not sufficient to be able to come to a clear conclusion on this point and the deeper discernment in managing habits in the company is unfortunately not available.

A subjective evaluation of Survey 1 seems to display that on average, there is a low learning disability in the company.

The next step in this issue was to find out the reasons for these learning disabilities as well as their impact on

---

1 cf. App. C.

company results. This information is important to promote change towards a learning and nonviolent culture.

Index

Acceptance... .56, 59, 129, 131 f.
Aggressive behavior..............41
Alt.........................49, 133
Andrews................................133
Annan, Kofi...........................25
Appreciation......29, 56, 59, 76, 86, 129
Argyl....................................83
Arnold Toynbee.....................25
Artifacts..............................15 f.
Arun Gandhi.................48, 100
Autogenic Training...............37
Autonomy..............................63
Balzert............................133, 143
Bancke................................133
Basic assumptions... 14 ff., 109, 113
Basic assumptions'.................70
Bauer......................................62
Behavior.....14, 18, 22 f., 35, 41, 99, 108 f., 118, 173
Behrend..........................26, 133
Being..26, 50, 101, 103, 133, 174
Bihl..134
Bittelmeyer..........................134
Blame.......53, 106 ff., 115 f., 180
Blaming........................108, 115
Boiled frog, the parable of.. ....182 f.
Bolzen..........................25, 134
Bruhn..........................102, 134
Burke..........................64, 134

Bußmann.........46, 124, 134, 137
Campbell, Converse and Willard...............................83
Carnegie....................47, 134
Childhood.............................36
Christian.............................120
Collectivism..........................23
Collins.......................74, 134
Commitment...............78, 117
Communication....31, 46 f., 55, 99, 106 ff., 113 f., 116 f., 124, 126 ff., 144, 161 f., 176
Compassion...........45, 56 f., 107
Competition.....60, 74, 98, 120, 124, 180, 182
Competitiveness............17, 137
Conflict... 25, 42, 53, 56, 96, 104 ff., 112, 140, 185
Conflict-.............................185
Conscience...............43 f., 89, 97
Conviction...................78 f., 128
Cornelia.............................134
Corporate Social Responsibility....................131
Covey......63, 70 f., 73, 76, 78 f., 89, 95 ff., 117, 122, 135
Crime.............................48, 90
Crisis.....17, 25, 29, 34, 38 f., 44, 94, 126, 177, 180 ff.
Criticism.....22, 35, 75, 109, 114 ff.

Culture.. 1, 9 ff., 13 ff., 23 f., 27, 32, 34 ff., 59, 62 ff., 66, 69 f., 72 f., 76, 79 f., 88, 90, 92 f., 96, 99 f., 103, 105, 107, 112 f., 116, 119, 125, 127 ff., 132, 136 f., 139, 143, 176, 184 ff.
Culture issues ... 39
Darwin ... 62
David and Goliath ... 96
Davis ... 14, 139
Dawtry ... 90, 135
Deadly Sins ... 43, 48
Deal ... 17 f., 20, 38, 135, 176
Deal and Kennedy ... 17 f., 38
Deal and Kennedy' ... 20
Decision-making ... 20, 35, 63, 79, 126, 174
Definition ... 14, 29, 34, 36 f., 41 f., 48, 55, 65, 70 ff., 75, 77, 125, 127, 161, 179, 181
Dimensions of culture ... 10, 21
Dominance strategies ... 53 f.
Drosdek ... 79, 113, 127 ff., 135, 143
Drucker .. 33 f., 71, 73 f., 89, 135, 140
Dunn ... 135 f.
Easterlin ... 84
Economic crisis ... 38, 44
Effort and gain model ... 86 f.
Egyptian ... 135
EKS-method ... 46
Emotional engagement ... 27 ff.
Emotional violence ... 51, 54
Empathy ... 57, 106, 111 f., 115, 126, 128, 161
Employability ... 126, 133
Empowerment ... 95
Ende ... 112, 135

Engelking ... 32
Englander ... 41, 135
Enrollment ... 78
Entrepreneur ... 127
Environment ... 15, 17, 26, 33 f., 38, 48 f., 59, 63, 71 f., 75, 92 ff., 117, 131, 173, 182 f.
Equality ... 22, 53, 96, 109
Espoused Values ... 15 f.
Ethics ... 99, 131, 139
Evolution ... 62
Extremism ... 26, 45
Festl ... 26, 135
Fifth Discipline ... 119 f., 125, 139, 179
Forgiveness ... 64
Frith ... 35
Fritz ... 34 f., 135
Frost ... 37, 136
Gallup ... 27 ff., 112
Gandhi ... 11, 42 f., 45 ff., 54 ff., 61 ff., 88, 93, 99 f., 106, 108 f., 118 f., 128 f., 133, 136, 140
Gandhi, ... 76
Gandhi, Arun ... 48, 100
German language ... 47, 176
Geus ... 120
Gillett ... 25, 96, 136
Globalization ... 44, 137
Gölzner ... 71, 136
Greek history ... 120
Greenleaf ... 93 f., 136
Guidance ... 97
Haller ... 91, 102, 137
Handy ... 13, 62, 64, 70, 83, 96, 119, 127, 137
Harvey ... 47
Heim ... 26, 52 f., 62 f., 89, 104, 106, 109, 112, 115 f., 138

Index

Heim (.................................26
Henke..............................92, 137
Herzberg.....................81 f., 86
Hitt..................................71, 137
Hofstede........21 f., 36, 137, 176
Holistic........................13, 32
Holler............................42, 137
Hoskisson..........................137
Humanity....................43 f., 48
Hygiene factors..................81 f.
IGOS................................32, 38
Individualism........................23
Injustice................9, 33, 69, 89
Ireland................................137
Jay Cross.............................102
Judgement........47, 65, 128, 176
Jumpertz........102, 119, 124, 137
Justice................92, 94, 169, 174
Kennedy..................17 f., 38, 135
Kennedy'................................20
Kirchler........................121, 137
Kleine................27, 29 ff., 138
Knowledge.....13, 22, 25, 43 ff., 102, 127 f., 161, 184
Kofi A. Annan.........................25
KPMG............................104, 140
Kreuzhof...................88, 99, 138
Krishnamurti................128, 138
La Monica....................121, 138
Leader as designer...............122
Leader as Steward...............122
Leader as teacher.................122
Leadership....10, 36, 38, 69, 80, 93, 95 f., 99 ff., 107, 121 ff., 129, 132, 136, 138 f., 144, 173
Learning disability..125, 179 ff.
Learning from experience..............................183 f.

Learning organization..119 ff., 128 f., 139
Legitimate Power................136
Lennon....................................72
Lifestyle.................................95
Lindemann... 26, 52 f., 62 f., 89, 104, 106, 109, 112, 115 f., 138
Lindemann and Heim....26, 52 f., 62 f., 89, 104, 106, 109, 115 f.
Lindemann and Heim (........26
London School of Economics and Political Science...........83
Long-term orientation..........24
Lorenz.............80, 82, 86 f., 138
Love..55 f., 62, 76, 88, 108, 118, 120, 129, 136, 138
Loyalty..................................84
Loye, David.........................62
Lüpke..................................138
Lyberth..................13 f., 25, 138
Mager..................................140
Mahatma..48, 54 f., 57 f., 61, 63, 93, 106, 119, 133
Management......23 f., 30 f., 35, 38 f., 50, 81, 85, 104, 121, 123, 135, 137 f., 143 f., 185
Manager....29, 75, 95, 121, 124, 135, 140, 175 f.
Manipulation......................121
Marcic....................76, 88, 138
Martin Luther King.........57, 93
Masculinity − femininity......24
Maslow...........................80, 84
Mewes............................46, 134
Militarism.............................25
Miller....................................33
Mission.................71 ff., 77, 92
Mission'................................71

Mistakes.. 64 ff., 96, 127, 175 f., 180
Mistrust....................57
Momo...............112, 135, 161
Money.. 27, 78, 82 ff., 91 f., 119, 126
Money,......................43
Moral... 43 ff., 52, 90, 92 f., 100, 118, 131, 138 f.
Motivating people..........80, 85
Motivation.. 11, 80 ff., 84 f., 88, 90, 109, 114, 134, 138
Motivational models............80
National culture...................21
Needs..11, 27, 42, 48, 57, 63, 78 ff., 82 ff., 95, 100, 105 ff., 122, 161, 173 f.
Negative capability.............127
Niebur........................139
Nietzsche......................70
Nink.........................28 ff.
Nonviolence.... 10 ff., 41, 48, 55 ff., 61 f., 73, 76, 88, 92, 104 f., 108, 119, 131 f., 162
Nonviolent.. 1, 10 ff., 25, 35, 46, 49, 55, 59, 62 ff., 69, 72, 76, 80, 88, 90 ff., 99 f., 105 ff., 116 f., 119, 125, 128 ff., 143 f., 161 f., 176, 186
Nonviolent communication.. 46, 55, 106 ff., 116 f., 128, 144, 161 f., 176
Nonviolent culture.. 1, 10 f., 35, 59, 62 ff., 69, 72, 76, 80, 88, 90, 92, 99 f., 105, 112 f., 116, 119, 125, 128, 130, 186
Observation........61, 110, 115 f., 125
Organization........................33

Organizational culture..10, 14, 17, 21, 24, 34 ff., 88, 99, 129, 132, 136, 139, 185
Organizations......9 ff., 14, 21 f., 26 f., 32, 34 ff., 43, 49, 73 f., 76, 78, 80, 88, 96, 109, 125, 127, 131, 138, 179 ff., 184
Orth......................65, 139
Osb Wien Consulting GmbH.. 124
Performance.....11, 14, 27 f., 34, 94, 113, 122, 124, 132
Philosophy... 15, 74 ff., 99, 143, 176
Pickartz.......................139
Politics......9, 19, 43, 45, 99, 117, 139 f.
Power.....21 f., 49, 53, 58, 88 ff., 93, 96 f., 112, 118, 136, 169, 172
Power-distance.....................21
Principle-centered................95
Principle-Centered Leadership... 95 f., 100 f., 122, 135
Proactive...........57, 77, 119, 181
Productivity.. 30 f., 51, 114, 139
Proudfoot Consulting......30 f., 139
Psychological violence..........41
Psychology of Happiness......83
Pyramid of Influence..........101
Quality............21, 75, 77, 83, 94
Relationships.....34 f., 62 f., 100 f., 105, 107, 109, 174
Respect.. 24, 42, 56 f., 59, 63, 73, 106, 110, 116, 125, 129, 170, 172, 174

Index

Rosenberg........46 f., 57, 83, 89, 106 f., 109 f., 112, 139, 161, 176
Rosenstiel..............................134
Ruhlmann..............................139
RWE............................118 f., 137
Schein....14 f., 34, 36 f., 139, 176
Schonfield..............139, 169, 174
Schwartz................................139
Schwarz and Davis................14
Security......19, 83, 86, 97 f., 109
Senge......13, 32 f., 35, 69 ff., 78, 120 ff., 127, 129, 139, 179 ff.
Servant.........93 f., 103, 136, 169
Servant Leadership.......93, 136
Seven Deadly Sins.................43
Shared vision.....70 f., 73, 121 f.
Short-term orientation...........24
Simon................................33, 69
Sioux...47
Society......9 ff., 13, 23 ff., 32 ff., 38, 47, 51, 54, 56, 58 ff., 65 f., 72, 76, 88, 90, 92, 100, 122, 131 f., 139, 144
Socrates.......................113, 128 f.
Sokrates.........................135, 143
Spears....................................136
Steyler Bank....................92, 140
Stress.............18 f., 24, 50, 108 f.
Suicidal tendencies of society.. 25
Suicidal-ness of Militarism...25
Swaim.............................71, 140
Systemic structure..........35, 122

Terrorism........................25 f., 45
Theobald...............26, 82 ff., 140
Toynbee....................25, 96, 136
Transparency..................63, 117
Trusteeship.............................58
Truth.........25, 51, 57, 59 ff., 173
Uncertainty-avoidance......22 f.
Understanding......17, 50, 55 f., 59, 71 f., 89, 97, 105 f., 110 ff., 114 f., 119 f., 123 f., 127, 129, 135, 169, 172, 177, 185
Unique Selling Proposition.. 46
Unison................................49 f.
United Nations......................25
US Ministry of Foreign Affairs...................................25
USP..46
Violence... 9 ff., 26, 41 ff., 45 ff., 56 f., 59, 89 ff., 99, 106, 121, 132, 135 f., 140
Vision... 33, 69 ff., 77 ff., 95, 97, 121 ff., 129, 140, 179
Vision,.....................................78
Vrij..60
Wahl......................................140
War............25, 113, 135 f., 170
Warshaw................41 f., 49, 140
Weingart.........................64, 140
Western culture....................66
Wilber............................13, 140
Wimmer................................124
Wisdom..........................97, 138
Zittlau.. 50, 55 ff., 60 f., 99, 128, 140

www.ingramcontent.com/pod-product-compliance
Lightning Source LLC
LaVergne TN
LVHW032009070526
838202LV00059B/6371